STATE PUBLICATIONS

MEDWAY • GILLINGHAM

CHATHAM • ROCHESTER • STROOD

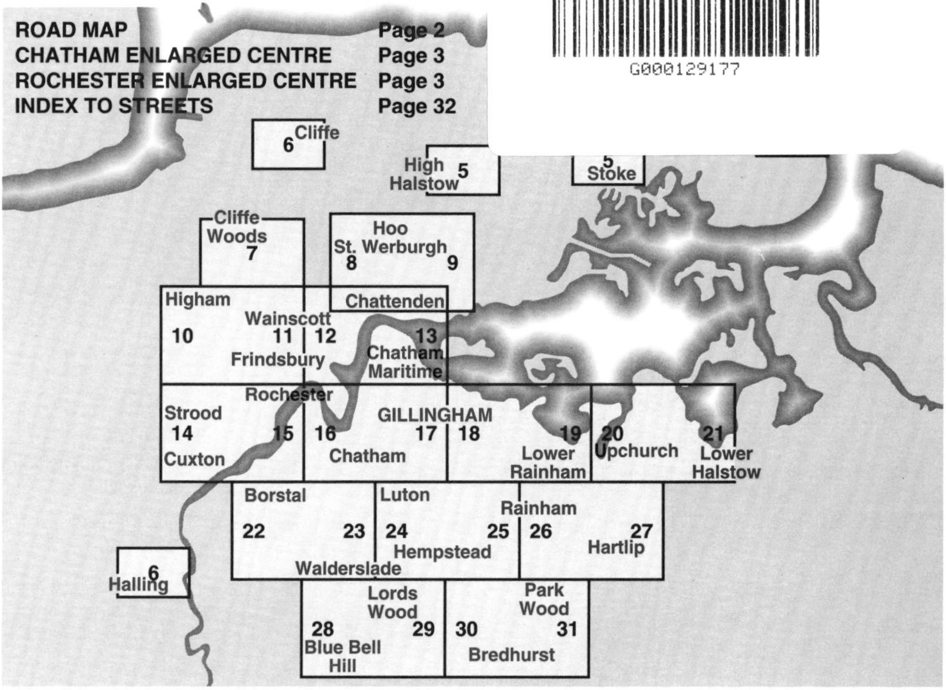

Every effort has been made to verify the accuracy of information in this book but the publishers cannot accept responsibility for expense or loss caused by an error or omission. Information that will be of assistance to the user of the maps will be welcomed.

The representation on these maps of a road, track or path is no evidence of the existence of a right of way.

Car Park	P
Public Convenience	C
Place of Worship	+
One-way Street	→
Pedestrianized	(hatched)
Post Office	●

Scale of street plans 4 inches to 1 mile
Unless otherwise stated

Street plans prepared and published by ESTATE PUBLICATIONS, Bridewell House, TENTERDEN, KENT, and based upon the ORDNANCE SURVEY mapping with the permission of The Controller of H. M. Stationery Office.

The Publishers acknowledge the co-operation of the local authorities of towns represented in this atlas.

Estate Publications 005 R

ISBN 1 84192 026 6

ROAD MAP

Scale: 3 Miles to 1 Inch

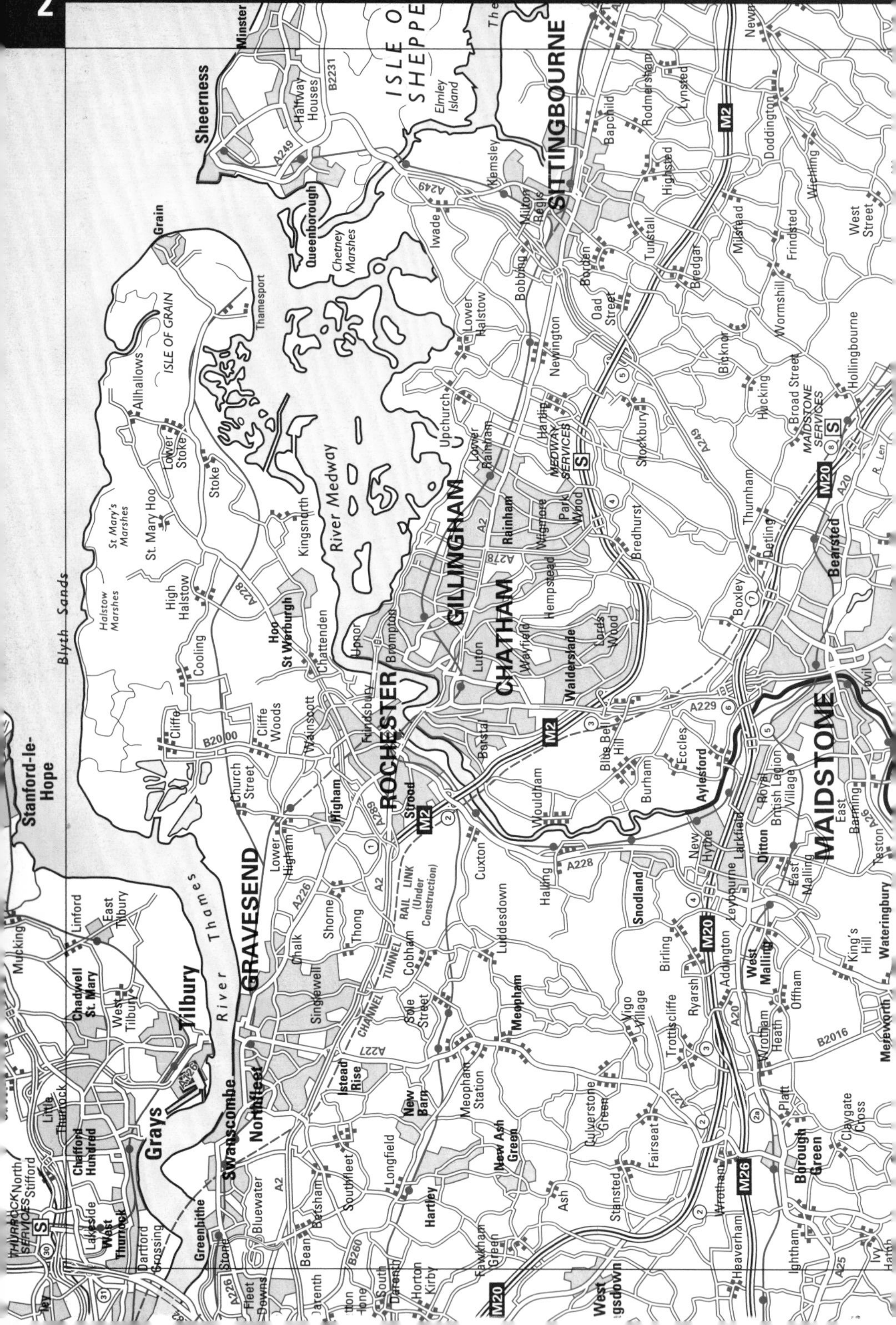

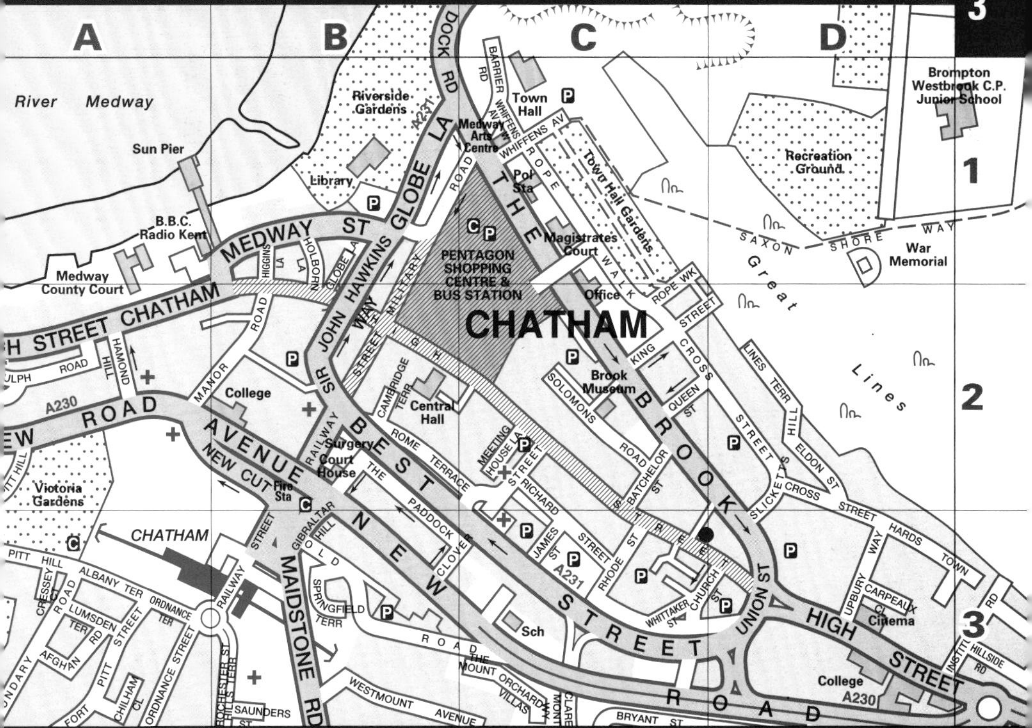
A
B
C
D
1
2
3
River Medway
Sun Pier
B.B.C. Radio Kent
Medway County Court
Riverside Gardens
Library
Town Hall
Medway Arts Centre
Pol Sta
Magistrates Court
Office
PENTAGON SHOPPING CENTRE & BUS STATION
CHATHAM
Brook Museum
Central Hall
College
Surgery
Court House
Fire Sta
Victoria Gardens
CHATHAM
Sch
Cinema
College
Brompton Westbrook C.P. Junior School
Recreation Ground
War Memorial
Town Hall Gardens
SAXON SHORE WAY
Great Lines
DOCK RD
BARRIER RD
WHIFFENS AV
GLOBE LA
A231
ROAD
THE
ROPE WALK
ROPE WK
STREET
MEDWAY ST
HIGGINS LA
HOLBORN LA
GLOBE LA
SIR JOHN HAWKINS WAY
MILITARY
HIGH STREET CHATHAM
ROAD
HAMOND HILL
ULPH ROAD
MANOR ROAD
A230
NEW ROAD
AVENUE
NEW CUT
RAILWAY ST
BEST
CAMBRIDGE TERR
ROME TERRACE
THE PADDOCK
CLOVER
MEETING HOUSE LA
STREET
RICHARD
JAMES ST
A231
STREET
NEW STREET
SOLOMONS ROAD
KING
CROSS
QUEEN ST
BATCHELOR ST
BROOK
RHODE ST
WHITTAKER ST
CHURCH ST
UNION ST
LINES TERR
HILL
ELDON ST
STREET
SLICKETTS
CROSS STREET
HARDS TOWN
WAY
UPBURY
CARPEAUX CL
HIGH STREET
RD
HILLSIDE RD
INSTITUTE
A230
ROAD
PITT HILL
ALBANY TER
ORDNANCE TER
CRESSEY
ROAD
LUMSDEN TER
RD
AFGHAN
PITT STREET
ORDNANCE STREET
FORT
CHILHAM CL
BOUNDARY
GIBRALTAR HILL
RAILWAY
MAIDSTONE RD
ROCHESTER ST
HILL TER
SAUNDERS ST
OLD ROAD
SPRINGFIELD TERR
THE MOUNT
ORCHARD VILLAS
WESTMOUNT AVENUE
MONT
CLARE
BRYANT ST
WITT HILL

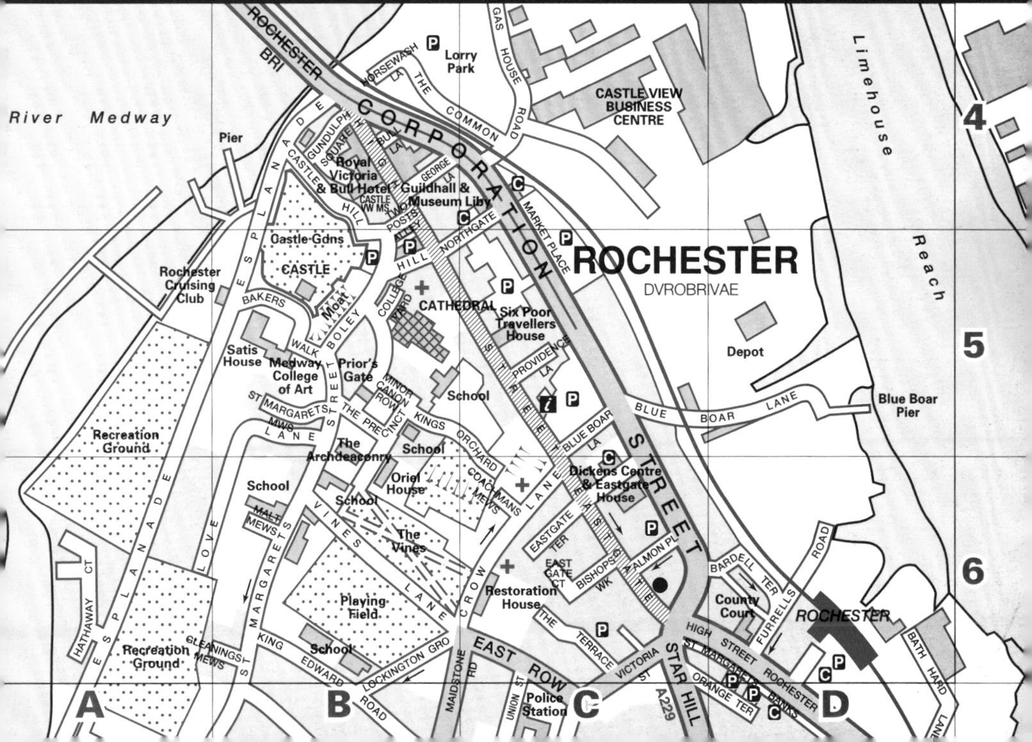
A
B
C
D
4
5
6
River Medway
ROCHESTER BRI
Pier
Rochester Cruising Club
Recreation Ground
Recreation Ground
Lorry Park
CASTLE VIEW BUSINESS CENTRE
Royal Victoria & Bull Hotel
Guildhall & Museum Liby
Castle Gdns
CASTLE
Moat
CATHEDRAL
Satis House
Medway College of Art
Prior's Gate
Six Poor Travellers House
ROCHESTER
DVROBRIVAE
Depot
School
The Archdeaconry
School
Oriel House
School
School
The Vines
Playing Field
School
Dickens Centre & Eastgate House
Restoration House
County Court
Blue Boar Pier
ROCHESTER
Police Station
Limehouse Reach
HORSEWASH LA
THE COMMON
GAS HOUSE ROAD
CORPORATION
GUNDULPH SQUARE
BULL LA
GEORGE LA
CASTLE HILL
CASTLE VW MS
TWO POSTS ALLEY
NORTHGATE
MARKET PLACE
ESPLANADE
BAKERS WALK
BOLEY HILL
COLLEGE YARD
HIGH
STREET
PROVIDENCE LA
MINOR CANON ROW
ST MARGARETS MWS
THE PRECINCT
KINGS ORCHARD
BLUE BOAR LANE
BLUE BOAR LA
COACHMANS MEWS
LANE
STREET
EASTGATE TER
EAST GATE CT
BISHOPS WK
ALMON PL
MALT MEWS
VINES LANE
CROW LANE
LOVE LANE
ST MARGARETS STREET
HATHAWAY CT
ESPLANADE
KING EDWARD ROAD
CLEANINGS MEWS
LOCKINGTON GRO
MAIDSTONE RD
EAST ROW
UNION ST
THE TERRACE
VICTORIA ST
STAR HILL
A229
HIGH STREET ROCHESTER
ST MARGARETS BANKS
ORANGE TER
BARDELL TER
FURRELLS
ROAD
BATH HARD
LANE

ALLHALLOWS

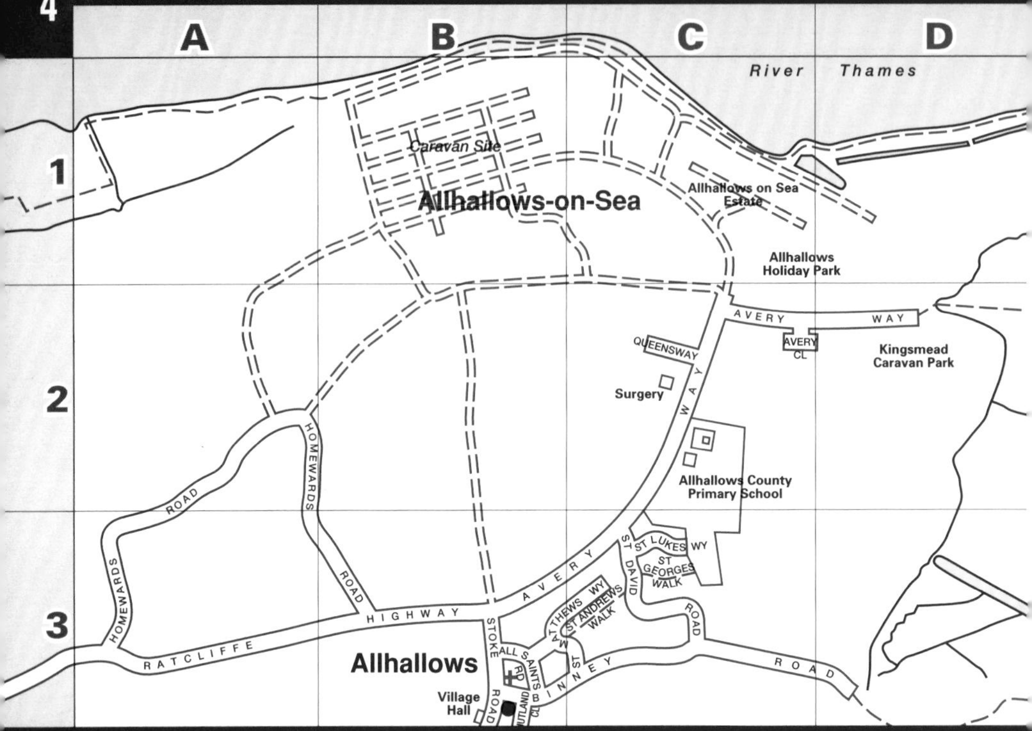

GRAIN

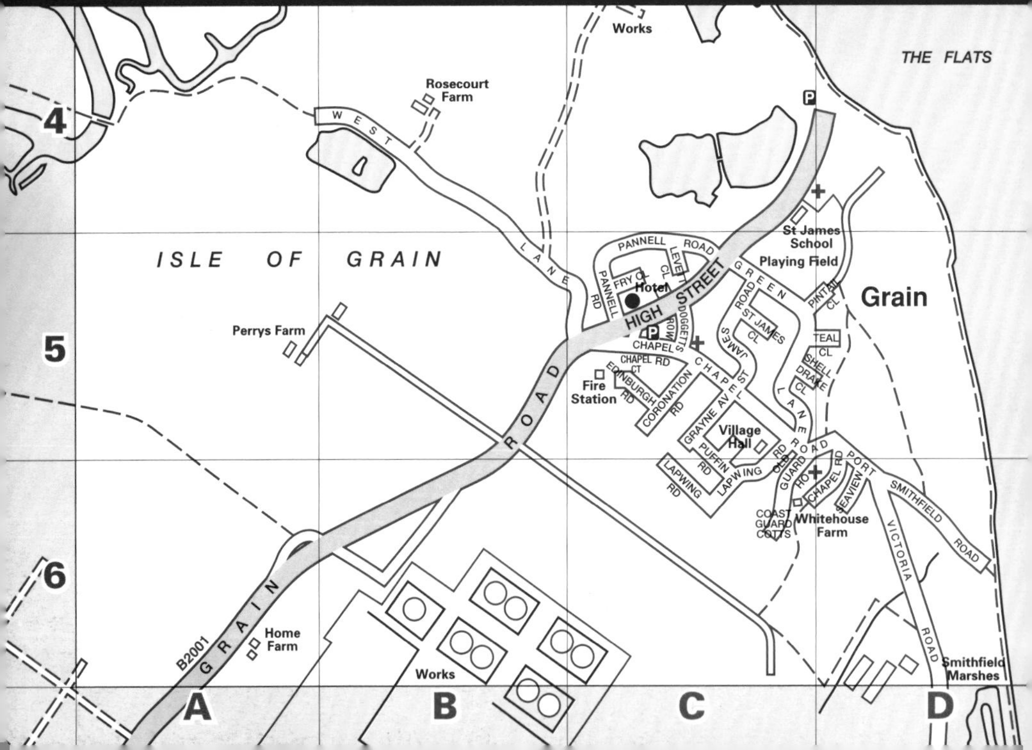

HIGH HALSTOW

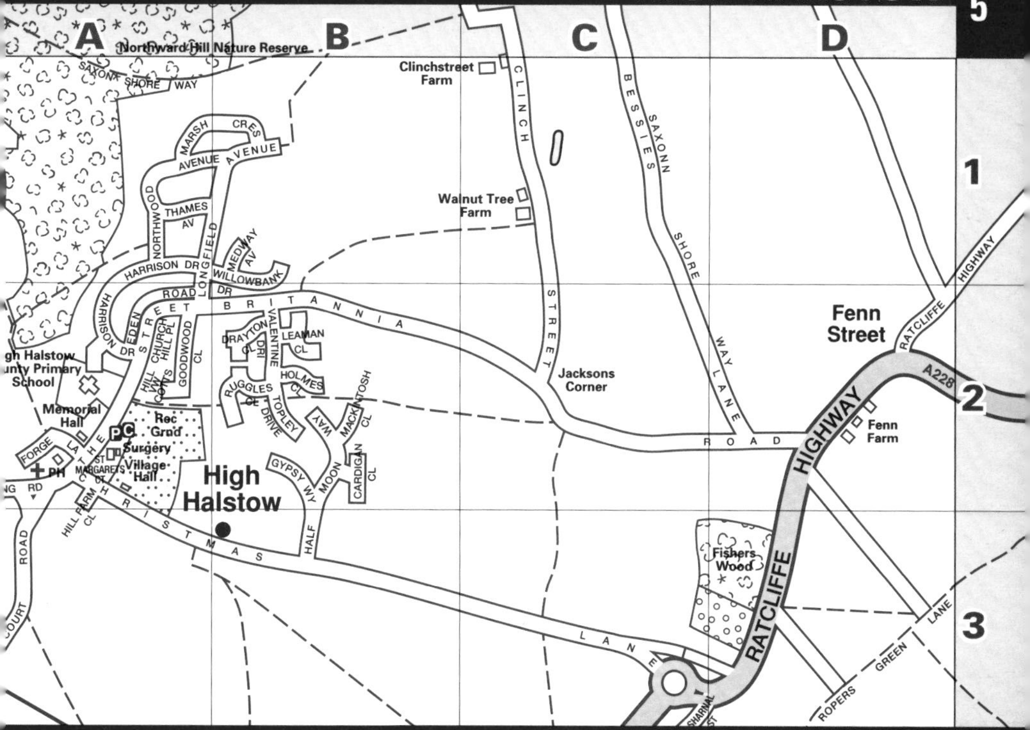

STOKE

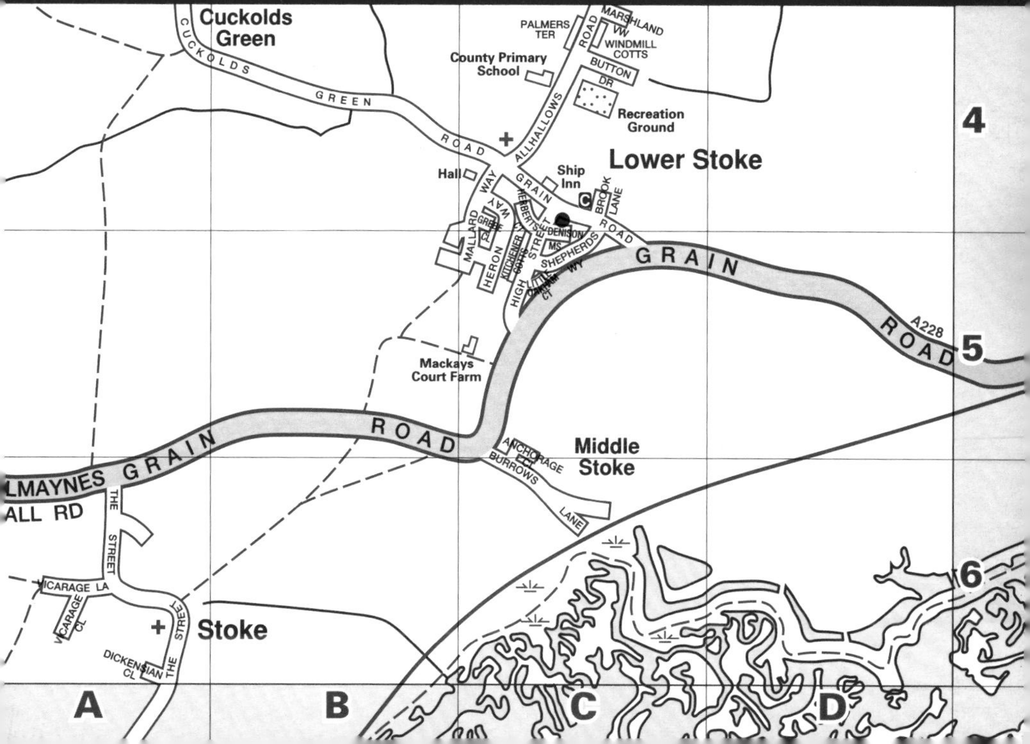

CLIFFE

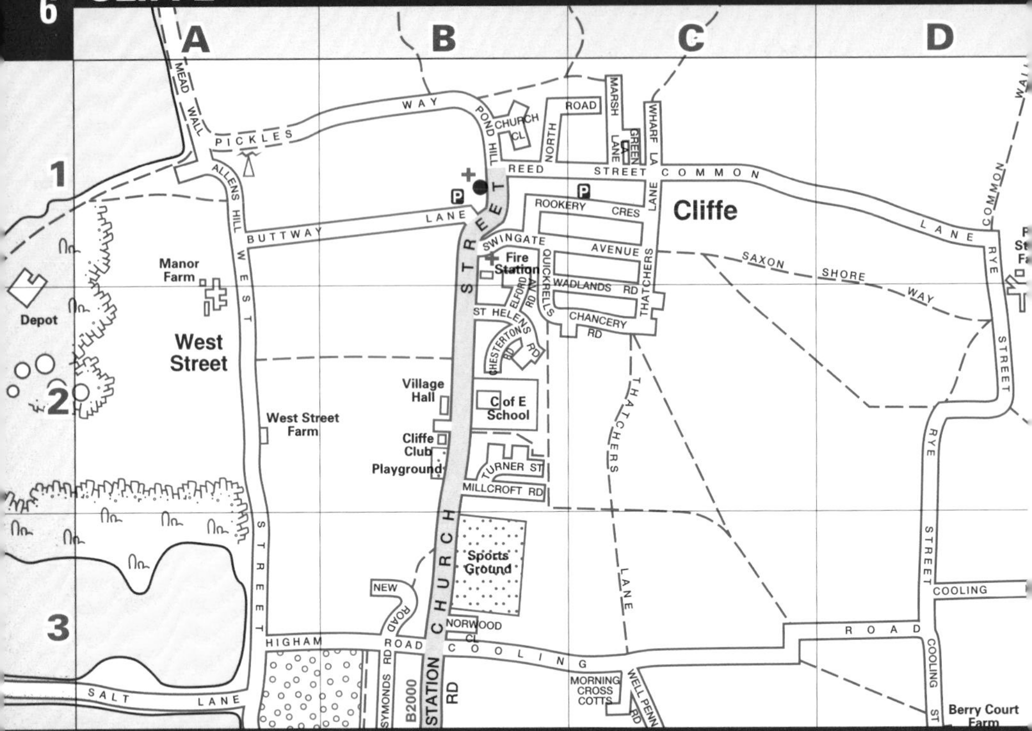

HALLING

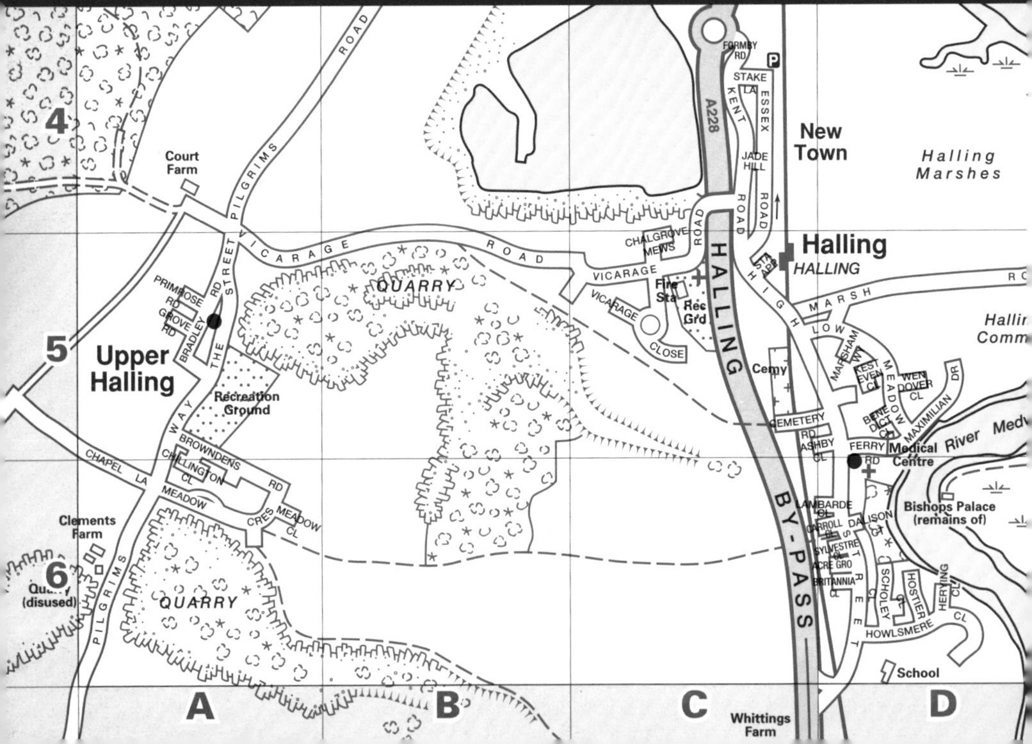

Cliffe Woods
Lee Green
Mockbeggar
Lower Higham
Gore Green
Little Oakleigh
Lillechurch Farm
White House Farm
Higham County Primary School
Higham Memorial Hall
Cliffe Woods County Primary School
Church Street
Reservoir
Reservoir
Rec Grnd
Comm Cen
HIGHAM
TOWN ROAD
RD B2000
MERRYBOYS ROAD
BUCKLAND ROAD
LILLECHURCH ROAD
GREEN LANE
BULL LANE
CHURCH STREET
LOWER ROAD
ROCHESTER ROAD
LANDWAY
SCHOOL LANE
CHALK ROAD
CANAL ROAD
SANDHILL LA
MARTINS CL
LAKE DR
THE ADELAIDE
REYNOLDS FIELDS
STEADMAN CL
TWOGATES HILL
BUNTERS HILL
LOWER ROAD
COMMON ROAD
HAVEN ROAD
LEE GREEN ROAD
HAM RIVER HILL
VIEW ROAD
MILTON AVENUE
LAKESIDE
WOODSIDE GREEN
TENNYSON AVENUE
DORCHESTER CL
NEWBURY CL
MORTIMERS AV
LADYCLOSE AV
MASEFIELD DR
SHAW CL
CARDENS RD
BATTLESMERE RD
WENTWORTH DR
MALLING DENE CL
PORT VIEW
WAY RD
REEDHAM CRES
RD GOODWIN ROAD
BREWER RD
ARCHER RD
BROOKMEAD CL
ENGLEFIELD CRES
HILTON RD
GRAVENEY CL
SEDLEY CL
ASHWOOD CL
HALE RD
THAMES
Ratley Wood
A
B
C
D
E
F
1
2
3
4
11

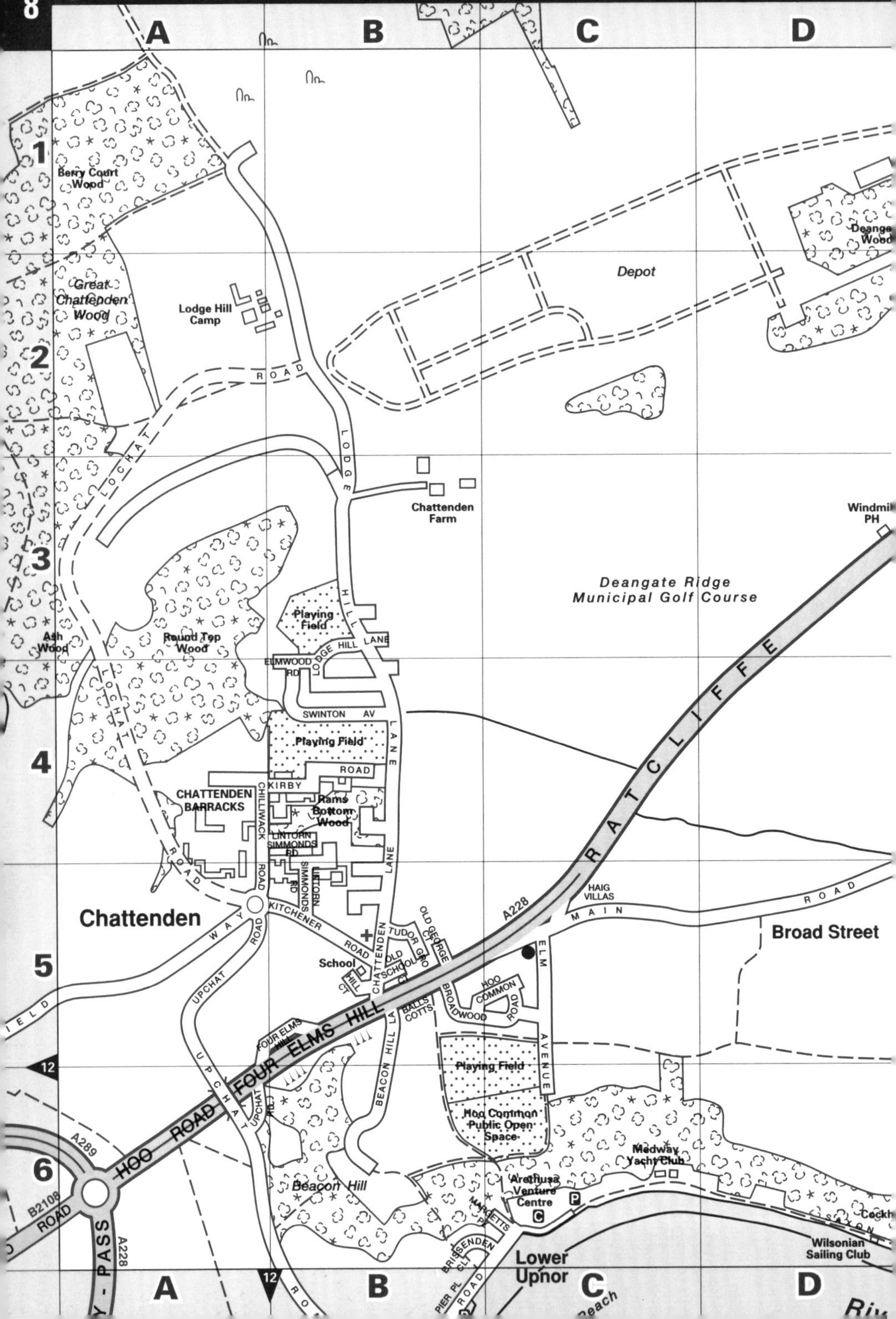
A
B
C
D
1
2
3
4
5
6
Berry Court Wood
Great Chattenden Wood
Lodge Hill Camp
ROAD
LOCHAT
LODGE
HILL
Depot
Deangate Wood
Chattenden Farm
Windmill PH
Deangate Ridge Municipal Golf Course
Playing Field
LODGE HILL LANE
ELMWOOD RD
Ash Wood
Round Top Wood
SWINTON AV
Playing Field
LANE
ROAD
KIRBY
CHATTENDEN BARRACKS
CHILLIWACK
Rams Bottom Wood
LINTORN SIMMONDS RD
SIMMONDS RD
LINTORN
RATCLIFFE
HAIG VILLAS
MAIN ROAD
A228
Chattenden
WAY
ROAD
KITCHENER ROAD
School
CHATTENDEN
TUDOR GRO
OLD GEORGE CT
OLD SCHOOL CT
HILL CT
ELM
Broad Street
HOO COMMON ROAD
BROADWOOD
BALLS COTTS
FOUR ELMS HILL
UPCHAT
IELD
12
BEACON HILL LA
AVENUE
Playing Field
Hoo Common Public Open Space
Medway Yacht Club
A289
HOO ROAD
ROAD
B2108
Beacon Hill
Arethusa Venture Centre
P
C
MARGETTS PL
SAXON
Cockham
Wilsonian Sailing Club
BY-PASS
A228
BRISSENDEN CL
Lower Upnor
PIER PL
ROAD
Beach

E
F
G
H
1
2
3
4
5
6
13
Hoo St. Werburgh
A228
HIGHWAY
DUX COURT ROAD
Athletics Track
Tennis Courts
P
angate Ridge Sports Complex
Indoor Bowls
18 Hole Golf Pitch & Putt
Driving Range
ROPERS LANE
SAXON SHORE WAY
Sports Ground
Sports Ground
BLACKMAN CL
BELLS LANE
ROAD
Resr.
WALL CL
FOURWENTS
ROCHESTER CR
KINGSHILL
ROCHESTER CRES
LANE
Recreation Ground
WEBB CL
ROAD
STURDEE COTTS
ROAD
GRANDSIRE
BALFOUR RD
DRIVE
PANKHURST
LINTON DANN CL
MOREMENT RD
MARLEY RD
ROAD
VIDGEON AVENUE
ST JOHNS
WALTERS RD
GDNS
Medical Centre
KINGSNORTH CL
Street Farm
Yew Tree Lodge Residential Home
KNIGHTS
DRIVE
ROAD
AVELING CL
ROBSON
WYLIE
RD
ROAD
BELLS
KNIGHTS
MISKIN
KNIGHTS CL
ROAD
Hoo St Werburgh School
Hundred of Hoo School
POTTERY ROAD
Hall
Rec Ground
TRUBRIDGE
PEAL CL
Red Cross Centre
THE BUNGALOWS
HERDS DOWN
GORDON RD
KILLICK RD
NEWITT ROAD
COOMBE RD
ROAD
FLACK GDS
LANE
STOKE
JENNIFER CT
MAIN ST
CRES
CP
Pol Sta
ROAD
Swimming Pool
WERBURGH
Fire Station
TILLEY CL
Medical Centre
Village Institute
BROOK SIDE
CHURCH
NURSERY GDNS
BUTTIMAN CL
ABBOTS COURT ROAD
Library
WILLOW GRANGE
Day Centre
ARMYTAGE CL
EVEREST MEWS
EVEREST
DRIVE
STREET
VICARAGE
WHITE HOUSE CL
Sewage Works
St Werburgh
CHURCH FARM CL
SAXON SHORE WAY
Cockham Farm
LANE
Hoo Lodge
VICARAGE LA
SAXON SHORE WAY
Hoo Ness Yacht Club
Hoo Marina Park
Hundred of Hoo Sailing Club
SHORE WAY

A
B
C
D
1
2
3
4
5
6
Hill Farm
Higham Memorial Hal
7
Higham
Chilton Hills Wood
Chilton Hill
TAYLORS LANE
VICARAGE RW
HIGH VW
DICKENS CT
MOUNT BATTEN AV
SCHOOL LANE
ST JOHNS ROAD
ST JOHNS CL
Working Mens Club
FAIRVIEW DR
HIGHWOODS CL
DRIVE
GROVE
BEECH
CRESCENT
OAK
ASH
LANE ROAD
NORAH
WALMERS AVENUE
HOLLYTREE DR
BRIAR DALE
EVERGREEN CL
CARTON RD
CHILTON DR
DARBY GDNS
BRICE
DOMBEY CL
PEGGOTY CL
IRVINE RD
ROAD
HERMITAGE ROAD
THE BRAES
HILL
ELM CL
THE LARCHES
Telegraph Hill
Liby
HAYES CL
LANE
TELEGRAPH
FORGE LANE
Gadshill
GRAVESEND ROAD
A226
VILLA LANE
Court Wood
Starmore Wood
CHARLES DICKENS AV
COPPERFIELD CRES
Gadshill Farm
PEARTREE
CRUTCHES LANE
Great Crabbles Wood
BOWESDEN LANE
A289
COLEWOOD DR
WATLING STREET
A2
M2 JUNCTION 1
M2
14
Chapter Farm
Salters Cros Sports Grou
THE SHADES
PARKFIELDS
MILLFORDHOPE RD
CHETNEY CL
COPPERHOUSE DRIVE
YANTLET
SQUIRES CL
SHARFLEET DR
STANGATE
SWALE
ROAD
AVENUE
Chapter Girls School
CARNATION RD
Playing Field
The Bligh Primary School
Community Centre
BLIGH
Knights Place

E
F
G
H
7
B2000
TOWN RD
LOWER ROCHESTER ROAD
BUNTERS HILL
COMMON ROAD
LANE
ROAD
BUNTERS
1
Noke Street
HERMITAGE ROAD
DILLYWOOD
DILLYWOOD LANE
STONEHORSE LANE
STONEHORSE CT
2
12
A289
3
FORDWICH DR
HAWKENBURY RISE
HERTSFIELD AV
ROAD
HOLLYW
B2108
COOLING
LARKIN CL
WEAVERING
GRASMERE
GARDENIA CL
Temple Boys School
Playing Field
Bill Street
Little Hermitage
GRAVESEND ROAD
FARM
CLIFFE ROAD
LYNETTE AV
LYNORS AV
KING ARTHURS DRIVE
GODFREY CL
HYPERION DR
SAXON CL
HILLY FIELD CL
CHEQUERS CT
MERRYFIELD
SBRASTED CT
SMETHAM GDNS
HANCOCK CLOSE
WINDMILL
QUIXOTE CRES
CHATSWORTH DR
CHARTWELL CL
WINDMILL CL
YALDING CL
WEST ST
RANDOLPH COTTS
HILLTOP
BINGHAM
4
Hill Sch
BROMPTON FARM ROAD
HARLECH CL
WOODVIEW RISE
AVENUE
WESTERGATE RD
SANDY CROFT RD
ORCHARD AV
Recreation Ground
ROSEMOUNT CT
SHERBOURNE DR
CLARENDON
GARDENS
LYCHFIELD DR
MIDLAND DR
DONGOLA
EVEREST LA
MILL CL
RAVENSWOOD AV
PROSPECT AV
MAYFAIR
Fire Station
CARISBROOKE RD
FOUNTAIN RD
CONWAY CL
BEAUFORT RD
BROOM GORSE
Broom Hill Country Park
HATFIELD RD
SLATIN RD
BERBER RD
CROMER RD
GODDINGTON
Schoool
MILL POND CL
HILLSIDE AV
HONEYPOT CL
5
BURLEIGH CL
COURT ROAD
Abbey Court Sch
ABBEY ROAD
Broom Hill
BROMPTON ROAD
STEELE ST
MOORE ST
COLLIS ST
KITCHENER RD
CAMBRIDGE RD
ROMSEY CL
CLINTON AV
CRISPIN RD
RUSSETT CL
ALLINGTON
BRAMLEY RISE
DRIVE
WORCESTER CL
DUCHESS CL
DRAKES AV
WAY
MINERVA RD
BANNING ST
HONE ST
CROSS ST
HAYWARD AV
CECIL AV
FLORENCE ST
FRINDSBURY ROAD
STATION ROAD
BANKS
EVELYN
LINWOOD AVENUE
GADNAM CL
DEACON CL
LEYBOURNE
DEAN RD
A226
ROAD
SWAIN CL
NICHOLLS
Gordon School
Frindsbury
MARTIN RD
KEHAM
GROVE
BOWES RD
A2
WATLING STREET
CHAPTER RD
PEPYS
JERSEY
GORDON
BRYANT
WESTON
Youth Club
MONTFORT RD
MORGAN
GLANVILLE
STANHOPE
Health Centre
Sch
Medical Centre
ST MARYS RD
VICARAGE
GRANGE
VICTORIA
EASTERN
STH
ROAD
6
CENTRAL RD
CASTLE VW RD
St Nicholas School
BARTON
GUN LANE
EDWARD ST
NORTH ST
CHURCH PATH
BURGESS
ALBERT PL
COLUMBINE CL
LANCELOT AV
DAFFODIL RD
AVENUE
COBHAM CL
RIVER DRIVE
HARVEL AVENUE
C
Strood Sports Centre
Swimming Pool
DOWNSIDE
LONDON ROAD
HIGH STREET
FRIARY PL
MARSH ST
Westfield Business Centre
STOUR CLOSE
HUMBER CRES
WYATT PL
Rec Grd
ROAD
COMMERCIAL
TOLGATE LA
NEWARK YARD
DOGGETTS
KINGSWEAR GDNS
STROOD
WITHAM
MEWS
15
TINTAGEL CL
NORTHCOTE
ROAD
CHARLES ST
ALMA PL
ROACH ST
RD
Superstore
H
G
E
F
Elaine Av Junior School
CLIFTON
ELAINE
TINTAGEL GDS
DART
Tennis & Bowls Club
WOODSTOCK RD

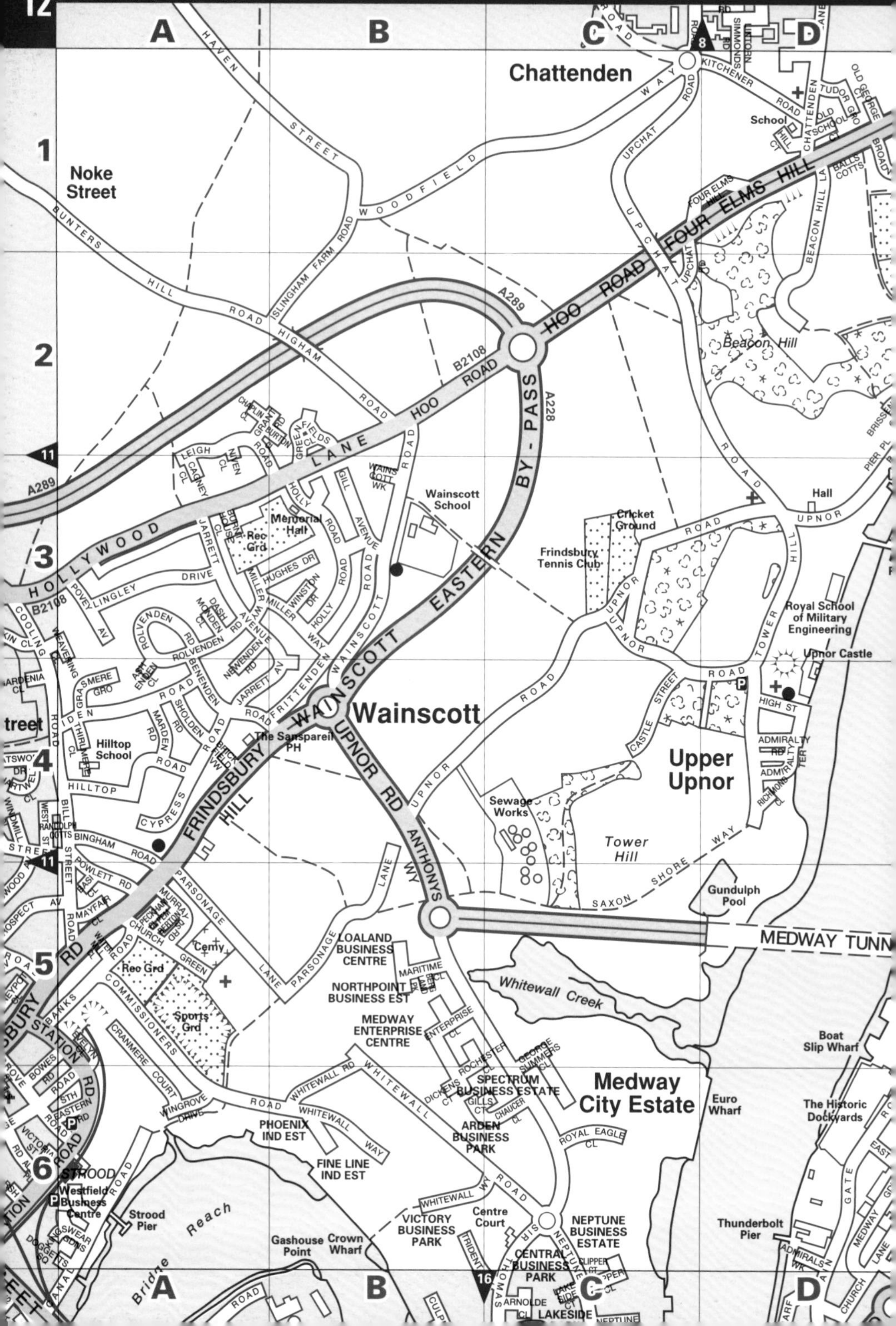
A
B
C
D
1
2
3
4
5
6
Chattenden
Noke Street
Wainscott
Upper Upnor
Medway City Estate
Beacon Hill
Tower Hill
Whitewall Creek
MEDWAY TUNN
HAVEN STREET
WOODFIELD WAY
ISLINGHAM FARM ROAD
BUNTERS HILL ROAD
HIGHAM ROAD
HOO ROAD
FOUR ELMS HILL
KITCHENER ROAD
UPCHAT ROAD
CHATTENDEN
BEACON HILL LA
A289
A228
B2108
LANE
HOLLYWOOD
EASTERN BY - PASS
WAINSCOTT
FRINDSBURY HILL
UPNOR RD
ANTHONYS WAY
UPNOR ROAD
TOWER HILL
CASTLE STREET
HIGH ST
ADMIRALTY RD
ADMIRALTY TER
SAXON SHORE WAY
Wainscott School
Memorial Hall
Rec Grd
Cricket Ground
Frindsbury Tennis Club
Hall
Royal School of Military Engineering
Upnor Castle
School
Hilltop School
The Sanspareil PH
Sewage Works
Gundulph Pool
LOALAND BUSINESS CENTRE
NORTHPOINT BUSINESS EST
MEDWAY ENTERPRISE CENTRE
SPECTRUM BUSINESS ESTATE
ARDEN BUSINESS PARK
PHOENIX IND EST
FINE LINE IND EST
VICTORY BUSINESS PARK
Centre Court
NEPTUNE BUSINESS ESTATE
CENTRAL BUSINESS PARK
LAKESIDE
Euro Wharf
Boat Slip Wharf
The Historic Dockyards
Thunderbolt Pier
Strood Pier
Gashouse Point
Crown Wharf
Reach
Cemy
Sports Grd
STROOD
Westfield Business Centre
WHITEWALL ROAD
WHITEWALL WAY
ROYAL EAGLE CL
SIR THOMAS
CHURCH GREEN
PARSONAGE LANE
COMMISSIONERS ROAD
CRANMERE COURT
WINGROVE DRIVE
STATION RD
BINGHAM ROAD
HILLTOP
CYPRESS
MARDEN ROAD
JARRETT AV
LINGLEY DRIVE
ROLVENDEN RD
BENENDEN
NEWENDEN RD
IDEN ROAD
HOLLY ROAD
GILL AVENUE
MILLER WAY
8
11
16

E
F
G
H
Broad Street
MAIN ROAD
Fire Station
Medical Centre
Village Institute
Day Centre
WILLOW GRANGE
EVEREST MEWS
ARMYTAGE CL
EVEREST DRIVE
ELM AVENUE
1
2
3
4
5
6
Cockham Farm
Hoo Lodge
SAXON SHORE WAY
Medway Yacht Club
Arethusa Venture Centre
Cockham Wood
Wilsonian Sailing Club
Hoo Ness Yacht Club
Lower Upnor
Upnor Reach
River Medway
Hoo Marina
Ford Marsh
Short Reach
Hoo Salt Marsh
Hoo Ness
Gillingham Reach
St Marys Island
Chatham Maritime
WEST ISLAND WAY
EAST ISLAND WAY
BRADFORDS CL
GOLDCREST DR
PARTRIDGE RISE
FOXTAIL CL
WOODRUSH PL
EGRET CL
WOODLARK RD
REDSHANK ROAD
THE CRAY
THE PINTAILS
HAVEN WAY
THE WHIMBRELS
SANDPIPER WAY
MARINE VW
BASIN 1
BASIN 2
Flagship Chatham
MARITIME WAY
Quayside House
Dock Square
Admiralty Place
Colonial Mutual
NORTH SIDE THREE ROAD
SOUTH SIDE THREE ROAD
GATE ROAD
END ROAD
EAST
Medway (Chatham) Dock Company
Bull Nose
East Wharf
Gillingham Piers
Admiralty Pier
PIER APPROACH ROAD
PIER ROAD
A289
Council Offices Compass Centre
WESTERN AV
PEMBROKE RD
CENTRAL AVENUE
Natural Resource Institute
SOUTH ROAD
OFFICERS RD
UPPER EAST RD
LWR EAST RD
KHYBER ROAD
PASLEY ROAD
College
ST MARYS GDNS
ROYAL SOVEREIGN AV
JOHNSON AV
PURSER WAY
BARRACKS
PRINCESS MARY AV
MEDWAY ROAD CAMP
CUMBERLAND RD
KELLY DR
LAUREL RD
BRIDGE RD
WHARF RD
BROMPTON BARRACKS
FIELDWORKS RD
Museum
Royal School of Military Engineering
Royal Engineers Museum
NORTH ROAD
GIBRALTAR AV
MEDWAY ROAD
VIRGINIA RD
KING WILLIAM RD
SIDNEY RD
MILBURN RD
EXMOUTH RD
ROSEBERY ROAD
LESLIE ROAD
TENDEN RD
ST ANDREWS RD
CAMDEN RD
SELBOURNE RD
BADEN RD
MILNER ROAD
HAMILTON
DEVON SHIRE RD
ST ALBANS CL
17
9

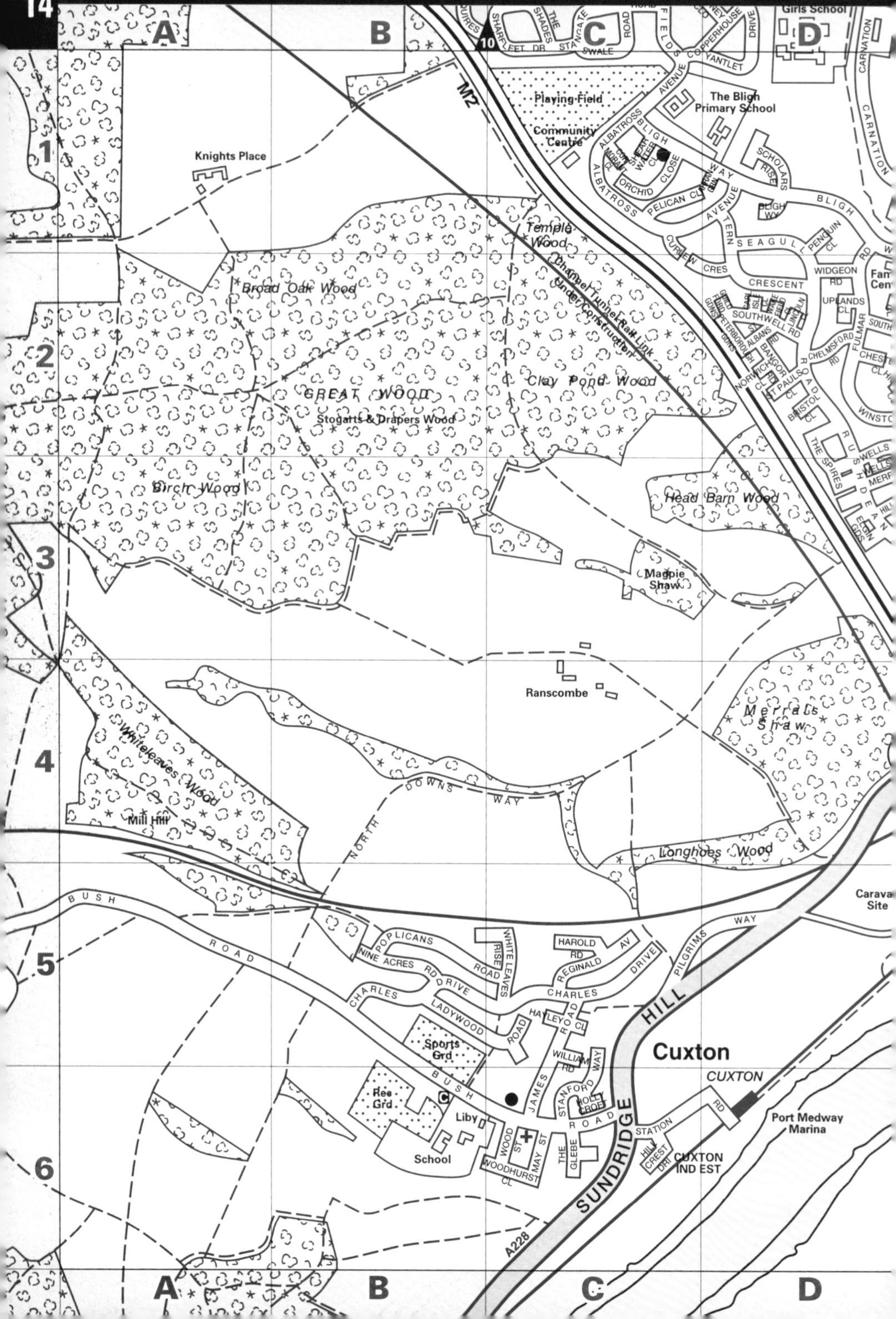
A
B
C
D
1
2
3
4
5
6
Girls School
M2
10
Playing Field
Community Centre
The Bligh Primary School
Knights Place
Temple Wood
Channel Tunnel Rail Link Under Construction
Broad Oak Wood
GREAT WOOD
Stogarts & Drapers Wood
Clay Pond Wood
Birch Wood
Head Barn Wood
Magpie Shaw
Ranscombe
Merrals Shaw
Whiteleaves Wood
Mill Hill
NORTH DOWNS WAY
Longhoes Wood
Caravan Site
BUSH ROAD
POPLICANS
NINE ACRES RD
WHITE LEAVES RISE
HAROLD RD
REGINALD AV
DRIVE
PILGRIMS WAY
CHARLES DRIVE
LADYWOOD ROAD
HAYLEY CL
WILLIAM RD
JAMES
STANFORD WAY
HOLLY CROFT
Sports Grd
Rec Grd
Liby
School
WOOD ST
MAY ST
WOODHURST CL
THE GLEBE
SUNDRIDGE HILL
Cuxton
CUXTON
STATION RD
HILL CREST DRI
CUXTON IND EST
Port Medway Marina
A228
ALBATROSS AVENUE
BLIGH WAY
ORCHID CLOSE
PELICAN CL
TERN
SEAGULL
PENGUIN CL
WIDGEON RD
CURLEW CRES
CRESCENT
UPLANDS CL
SOUTHWELL RD
ST ALBANS
BANGOR
NORWICH CL
ST PAULS CL
BRISTOL CL
CHELMSFORD RD
FULMAR
THE SPIRES
RUSHDEAN
WELLS
ELGIN GDNS
SCHOLARS RISE
CARNATION
COPPERHOUSE
YANTLET
DRIVE
SWALE
STANGATE
THE SHADES
SHARFLEET DR
ROAD
FIELDS

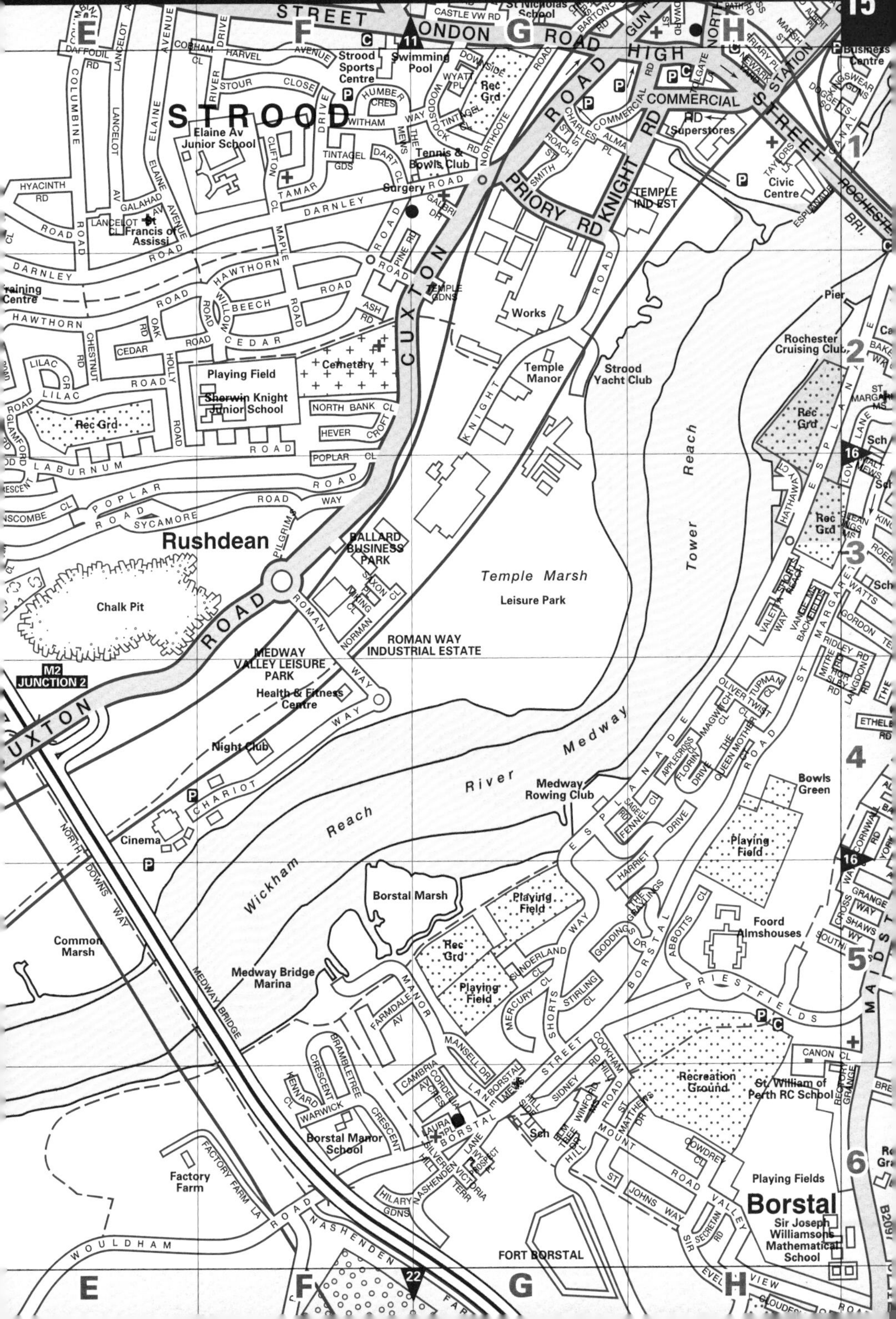
STROOD
Rushdean
Borstal
Strood Sports Centre
Swimming Pool
Elaine Av Junior School
Tennis & Bowls Club
Surgery
St Francis of Assissi
Training Centre
Playing Field
Sherwin Knight Junior School
Cemetery
Rec Grd
Chalk Pit
M2 JUNCTION 2
BALLARD BUSINESS PARK
MEDWAY VALLEY LEISURE PARK
Health & Fitness Centre
Night Club
Cinema
ROMAN WAY INDUSTRIAL ESTATE
Temple Marsh
Leisure Park
Works
Temple Manor
Strood Yacht Club
TEMPLE IND EST
Superstores
Civic Centre
Business Centre
Pier
Rochester Cruising Club
Tower Reach
River Medway
Reach
Wickham
Medway Rowing Club
Borstal Marsh
Common Marsh
Medway Bridge Marina
Factory Farm
Borstal Manor School
Foord Almshouses
Bowls Green
Recreation Ground
St William of Perth RC School
Playing Fields
Sir Joseph Williamsons Mathematical School
FORT BORSTAL
LONDON ROAD
HIGH STREET
COMMERCIAL RD
CUXTON ROAD
PRIORY RD
KNIGHT RD
DARNLEY ROAD
HAWTHORN ROAD
CEDAR ROAD
LABURNUM ROAD
POPLAR ROAD
SYCAMORE
ROMAN WAY
CHARIOT WAY
ESPLANADE
ST MARGARETS ST
BORSTAL ROAD
BORSTAL STREET
MANOR LANE
PRIESTFIELDS
NORTH DOWNS WAY
MEDWAY BRIDGE
WOULDHAM ROAD
NASHENDEN FARM
MAIDSTONE
B2097
E
F
G
H
1
2
3
4
5
6
11
16
22

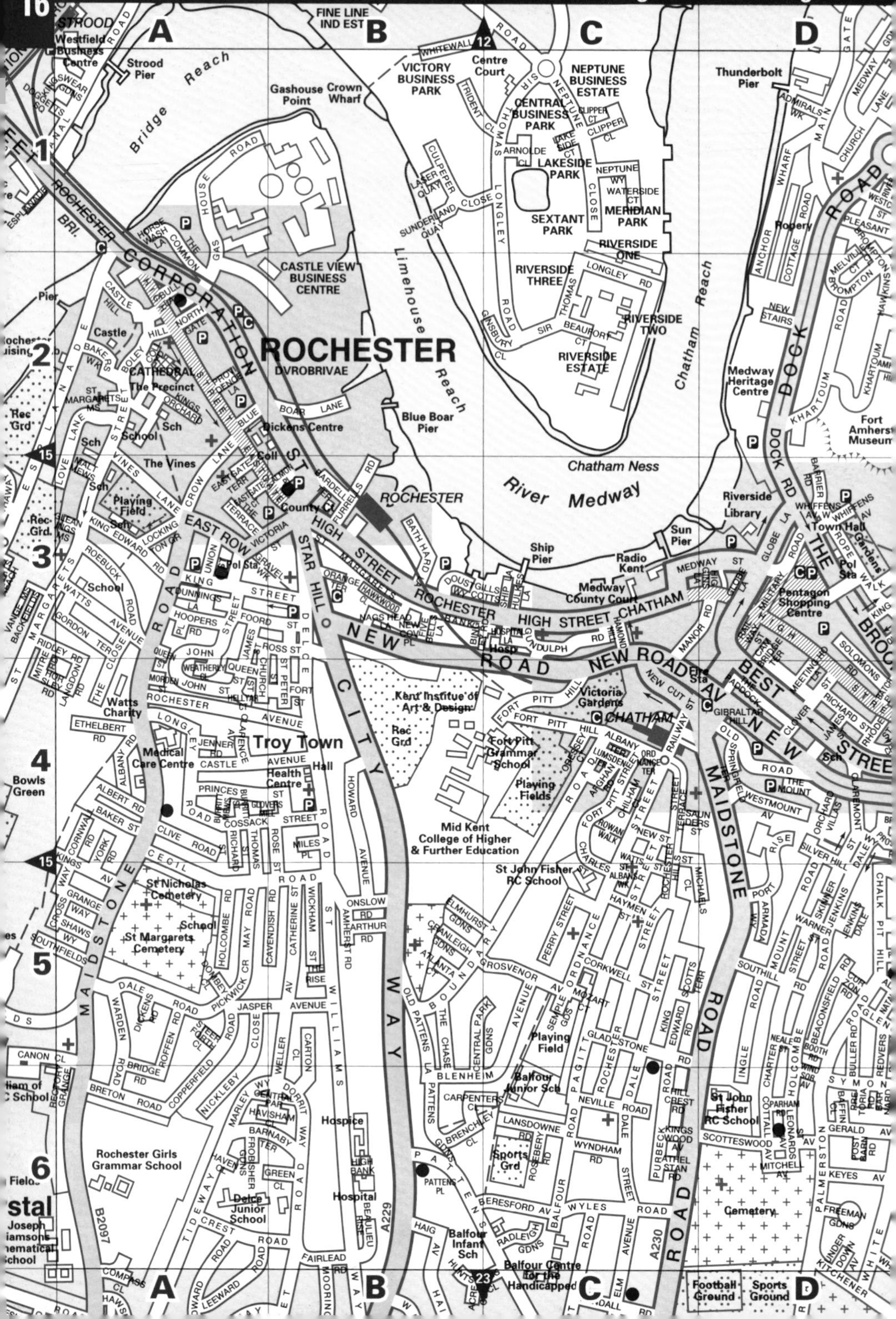
A
B
C
D
1
2
3
4
5
6
ROCHESTER
DVROBRIVAE
River Medway
Chatham Reach
Limehouse Reach
Bridge Reach
Chatham Ness
STROOD
Westfield Business Centre
Strood Pier
FINE LINE IND EST
Gashouse Point
Crown Wharf
VICTORY BUSINESS PARK
Centre Court
NEPTUNE BUSINESS ESTATE
CENTRAL BUSINESS PARK
LAKESIDE PARK
SEXTANT PARK
MERIDIAN PARK
RIVERSIDE ONE
RIVERSIDE TWO
RIVERSIDE THREE
RIVERSIDE ESTATE
CASTLE VIEW BUSINESS CENTRE
Thunderbolt Pier
Blue Boar Pier
Dickens Centre
Castle
CATHEDRAL
The Precinct
The Vines
Playing Field
County Ct
Sun Pier
Ship Pier
Radio Kent
Medway County Court
Riverside Library
Town Hall
Pentagon Shopping Centre
Medway Heritage Centre
Fort Amherst Museum
Troy Town
Watts Charity
Medical Care Centre
Health Centre
Kent Institute of Art & Design
Rec Grd
Fort Pitt Grammar School
Playing Fields
Mid Kent College of Higher & Further Education
St John Fisher RC School
Victoria Gardens
CHATHAM
St Nicholas Cemetery
St Margarets Cemetery
Rochester Girls Grammar School
Delce Junior School
Hospice
Hospital
Balfour Junior Sch
Balfour Infant Sch
Balfour Centre for the Handicapped
Sports Grd
Cemetery
Football Ground
Sports Ground
Bowls Green
CORPORATION
HIGH STREET
ROCHESTER HIGH STREET CHATHAM
NEW ROAD
CITY WAY
STAR HILL
MAIDSTONE ROAD
DOCK ROAD
THE BROOK
NEW STREET
BEST AV
A229
A230
B2097
12
15
23

E
F
G
H
1
2
3
4
5
6
BROMPTON BARRACKS
BARRACKS
MEDWAY ROAD CAMP
Museum
Royal School of Military Engineering
Royal Engineers Museum
Playing Field
Black Lion Field
Night Club
Hotel
Sports Centre
Swimming Pool
Sports Ground
Gymnasium
NAAFI
Brompton
Cricket Ground
Sports Ground
Rec. Grd
Football Ground
Brompton Westbrook C.P. Junior School
Rec Grd
War Memorial
Playing Field
Training Centre
Upbury Manor Secondary School
Great Lines
Saxon Shore Way
CHATHAM
Playing Field
Cinema
College
MEDWAY HOSPITAL
Accident Centre
Surgery
Sch
ALL SAINTS HOSPITAL
Arden Schs
Hillyfields Junior School
St Marys RCP Sch
INDUSTRIAL PARK
GILLINGHAM
Fire Station
Bus Station
Schools
Priestfield Stadium Gillingham F.C.
Maternity Hosp
Playing Field
Gillingham Park
Council Offices
School
School
Playing Field
Fire Station
Sch
School
Rec Grd
Luton
Upper
INDUSTRIAL
istchurch h School
PIER ROAD
A289
A2
BROMPTON ROAD
PRINCE ARTHUR ROAD
MEDWAY ROAD
CHATHAM HILL
RAINHAM RD
NELSON ROAD
DUNCAN RD
JEFFERY ST
HIGH ST
CANTERBURY STREET
GILLINGHAM ROAD
MARLBOROUGH ROAD
YORK AVENUE
LUTON ROAD
BEACON ROAD
CASTLE AVENUE
WINDMILL ROAD
SKINNER STREET
RAILWAY STREET
BALMORAL RD
FRANKLIN ROAD
PRIESTFIELD RD
LIVINGSTONE ROAD
CARLTON AV
ALEXANDRA AV
JUNCTION ROAD
OXFORD ROAD
SEATON ROAD
WATLING AV
OSPREY AV
KINGSWAY
13
18
18
24

A
B
C
D
Gillingham Marshes
Medway Cruising Club
Cinque Port Marshes
Miniature Golf Course
PIER ROAD
GADS HILL
Cemetery
Sports Ground
Grange
LOWER RAINHAM
SAXON SHORE WAY
Walnut Tree Farm
Grange Farm
Sports Hall
Grench Manor
GILLINGHAM
Priestfield Stadium Gillingham F.C.
Lower Twydall
BEECHINGS WAY INDUSTRIAL CENTRE
Little London Farm
Rec Grd
Recreation Ground
Robert Napier Secondary School
Playing Field
Twydall
Golf Course
Featherby Schools
Benenden Manor
Liby
Gillingham Club House
Vinall Park
Danecourt ESN Day School
Twydall Schools
RC School
Sports Grnd
Sports Ground
Sports Grd
Super Stores
Superstore
Ice Bowl
WATLING STREET
LONDON ROAD
1
2
3
4
5
6
17
25

E
F
G
H
Ferol Peak
Marshes
Horrid Hill
Sharpes Green
Riverside Country Park
Visitor Centre
HORRID HILL
LANE
ROAD
Manor Farm
Manor Court
Rainham Creek
20
1
2
3
4
5
6
Bloors Wharf
BLOORS WHARF RD
COWSTEAD LA
LANE
LOWER
RAINHAM
ROAD
B2004
WEST MOTNEY WY
MOTNEY
MOTNEY HILL ROAD
Lower Rainham
BERENGRAVE LANE
Berengrave Lane Nature Reserve
BLOORS
LOWER
PUMP
ROLVENDEN AV
THORNHAM
EASTLING CL
BEECHINGS
DODDINGTON RD
AVENUE
LANE
TRURO CL
RIPON CL
LICHFIELD CL
HEREFORD CL
WAY
ELY CL
Thames View Infants & Junior Schools
Eastcourt
Rainham Mark Grammar School
Playing Field
CLOSE
NORFOLK CL
LANGDALE
DORSET SQ
BEDFORD AV
AVENUE
BLOORS
PEMBURY WY
CHESTFIELD CL
PENSHURST CL
THE WILLOWS
HIGH ELMS
HOLMOAKS
Cricket Ground
Swimming Pool
Splashes Leisure Park
Cozenton Park
CHILTON CT
COZENTON CL
26
CRANFORD CL
TUFTON
NORTHUMBERLAND
DEVON
AVENUE
RAINHAM
CHALKY BANK
ROYSTONS CL
WOOLDEYS ROAD
BROOMCROFT RD
BUSHMEADOW RD
CHILDSCROFT
DIGNALS CL
PARKFIELD
STREETFIELD RD
ROAD
MACKLANDS WY
COBDOWN GRO
LAMBOURNE PL
WAY
ELLISON
STATION ROAD
B2004
WILLIAM STREET
HENRY STREET
WAKELEY
TILBURY ROAD
FINWELL ROAD
TWYFORD CL
COODEN CL
WIVENHOE CL
GRANARY
ROAD

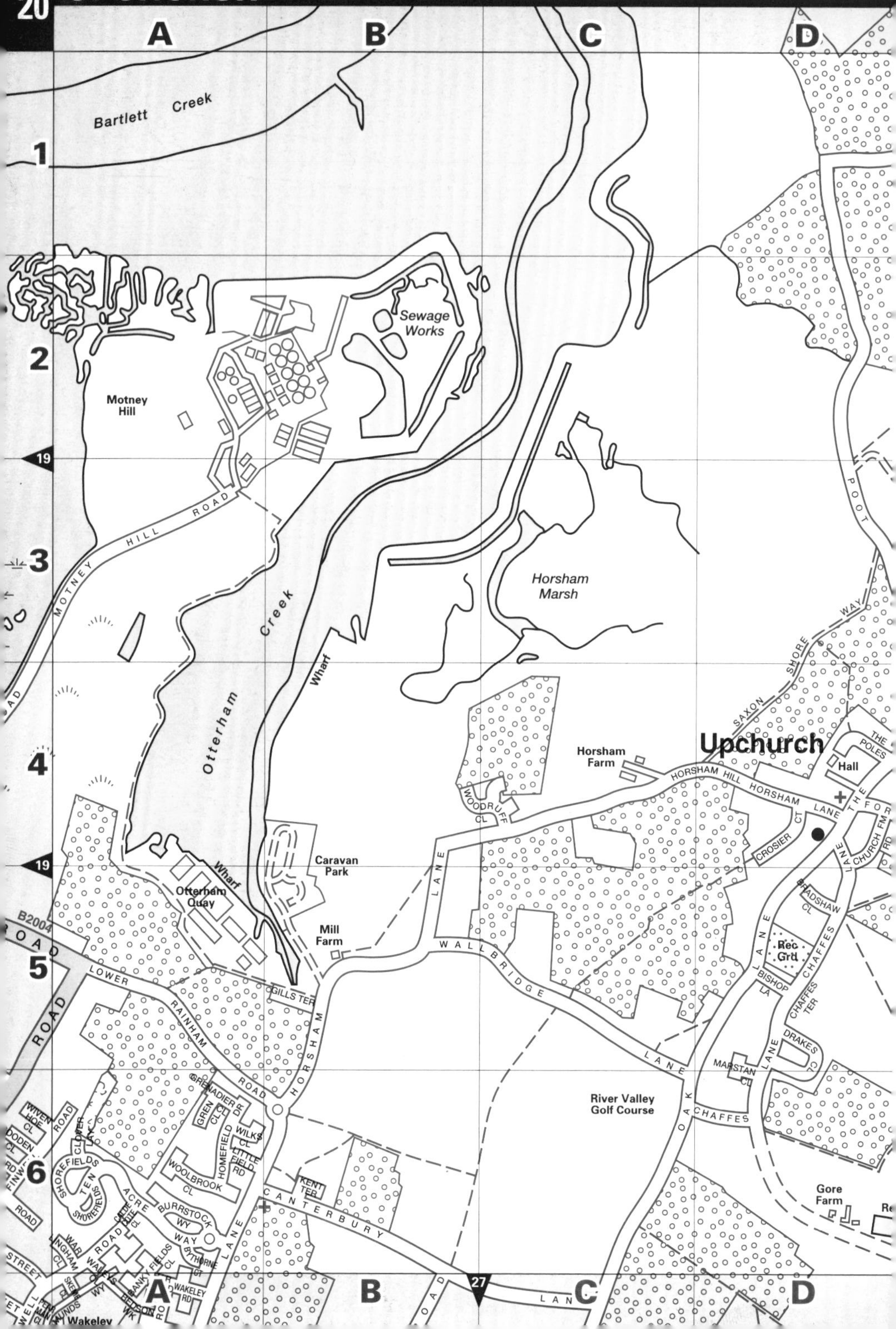
A
B
C
D
1
2
3
4
5
6
19
19
27
Bartlett Creek
Motney Hill
Sewage Works
MOTNEY HILL ROAD
Otterham Creek
Horsham Marsh
Wharf
Wharf
Caravan Park
Otterham Quay
Mill Farm
B2004
ROAD
LOWER RAINHAM ROAD
GILLS TER
HORSHAM LANE
WALLBRIDGE LANE
LANE
WOODRUFF CL
Horsham Farm
Upchurch
HORSHAM HILL
HORSHAM LANE
SAXON SHORE WAY
POOT LANE
THE POLES
Hall
THE FORGE
CROSIER CT
CHURCH FM RD
BRADSHAW CL
Rec Grd
CHAFFES LANE
BISHOP LA
CHAFFES TER
DRAKES CL
MARSTAN CL
OAK LANE
CHAFFES
River Valley Golf Course
Gore Farm
GRENADIER DR
GREEN CL
WILKS CL
HOMEFIELD DR
LITTLEFIELD RD
WOOLBROOK CL
KENT TER
CANTERBURY LANE
BURRSTOCK WY
SHOREFIELDS
TEN ACRE WAY
WIVENHOE CL
ROAD
WARLINGHAM CL
STREET
WAKELEY RD
Wakeley

E
F
G
H
1
2
3
4
5
6
Millfordhope
Saltings
Twinney Creek
Twinney
Saltings
Twinney
Wharf
Halstow Creek
Sewage
Works
HERON CL
CHURCH PATH
DRIVE
LAPWING
CURLEW
THE AV
THE GREEN
STREET
Lower
Halstow
VICARAGE
HILL
CROUCH
CT
WESTMORELAND
DRIVE
BURNTWICK DR
LA
Memorial
Hall
SCHOOL
SCHOOL
CUMBERLAND DR
LANE
WARDWELL
LANE
LANDRAIL RD
LANE
LANE
HALSTOW
Holywell
nty Primary
School
LANE HOLYWELL
LANE
Sports
Ground
Sports
Ground
Holywell
Farm
Home Farm
WESTFIELD COTTS
Primary
School
The
Laurels
BREACH
HOLYWELL
LANE
BOXTED
LA
LANE
am
een
E
F
G
H

A
B
C
D
1
2
3
4
5
6
15
School
Rochester Girls Grammar School
Playing Fields
Borstal
Sir Joseph Williamsons Mathematical School
FORT BORSTAL
NASHENDEN FARM LANE
Nashenden Farm
H.M. YOUTH CUSTODY CENTRE
H.M. PRISON COOKHAM WOOD
Playing Field
Res
Sports Grd
Playing Fields
East Cookham Wood
BRIDGEWOOD BUSINESS PK
Fort
The Stirling Centre
Sports Field
AIRPORT INDUSTRIAL ESTATE
Thomas Aveling School
Playing Field
ROCHESTER AIRPORT
MAIDSTONE ROAD
ROCHESTER ROAD
B2097
M2
Channel Tunnel Rail Link Under Construction
BURHAM ROAD
North Downs Way
Shoulder of Mutton Wood
Nine Acre Wood
Little Monk Wood
Well Wood
Barn Wood
Gorse Wood
Upper Nashenden Farm
Harris's Copse
Wouldham Common
HILL ROAD
MONK WOOD
Syle Wood
Middle Hill
LAKER ROAD
STONEY LANE
LANKESTER PARKER RD
SIR EVELYN ROAD
VALLEY VIEW ROAD
ST JOHNS WAY
SECRETAN RD
CLOUDESLEY RD
TREVALE RD
HORWOOD CL
MONKWOOD CL
BARNWOOD CL
SYLE WOOD CL
COOKHAM WOOD RD
PILOT RD
GALLEON CL
TIDEWAY
WAKE RD
BINNACLE RD
ARETHUSA RD
LEANDER RD
PENNANT RD
THE WARREN
ORION
EXETER WK
AJAX RD
COMPASS CL
HAWSER RD
THE FAIRWAY
WINDWARD RD
LEEWARD RD
THE ANCHOR
SPINNAKER CT
CREST RD
HILARY GDNS
NASHENDEN ROAD
VICTORIA TERR
PROSPECT PL
SILVER HILL
FACTORY FARM LA

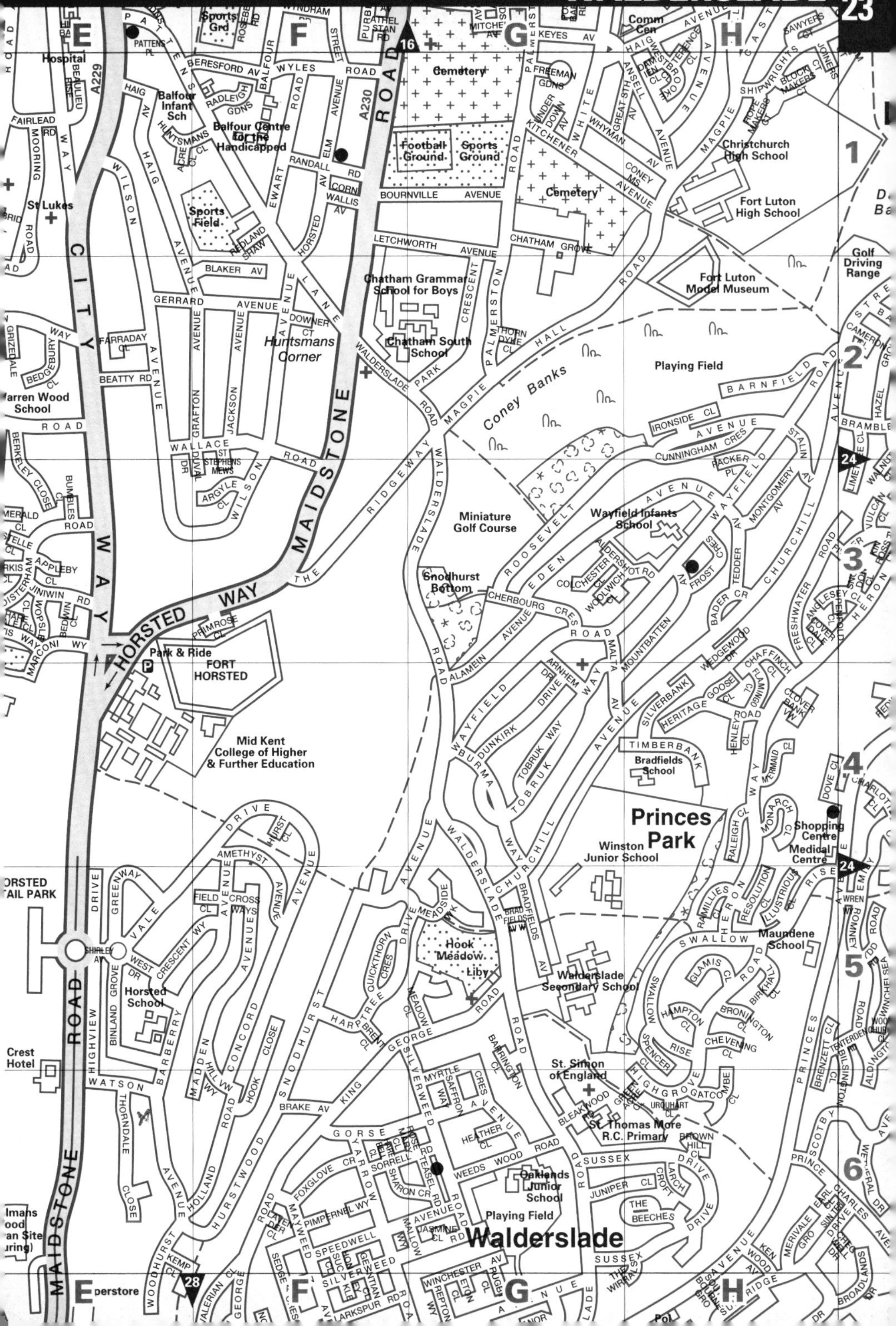
E
F
G
H
1
2
3
4
5
6
16
24
28
Hospital
St Lukes
Balfour Infant Sch
Balfour Centre for the Handicapped
Sports Grd
Sports Field
Cemetery
Football Ground
Sports Ground
Christchurch High School
Fort Luton High School
Fort Luton Model Museum
Golf Driving Range
Comm Cen
Chatham Grammar School for Boys
Chatham South School
Huntsmans Corner
Coney Banks
Playing Field
Warren Wood School
Miniature Golf Course
Wayfield Infants School
Snodhurst Bottom
Park & Ride
FORT HORSTED
Mid Kent College of Higher & Further Education
Princes Park
Winston Junior School
Bradfields School
Shopping Centre
Medical Centre
Maundene School
HORSTED RETAIL PARK
Horsted School
Crest Hotel
Hook Meadow
Liby
Walderslade Secondary School
St. Simon of England
St. Thomas More R.C. Primary
Oaklands Junior School
Playing Field
Walderslade
CITY WAY
MAIDSTONE ROAD
HORSTED WAY
A229
A230
WALDERSLADE ROAD
PRINCES AVENUE
CHURCHILL AVENUE
WEEDS WOOD ROAD
SNODHURST AVENUE
HURSTWOOD
KING GEORGE ROAD
MAGPIE HALL ROAD
BOURNVILLE AVENUE
LETCHWORTH AVENUE
GERRARD AVENUE
ROOSEVELT AVENUE
WAYFIELD ROAD
SWALLOW ROAD
SUSSEX DRIVE

A
B
C
D
1
2
3
4
5
6
17
23
29
Luton
Upper Luton
Hale
Darland
Wayfield
Capstone
East Hill
Daisy Banks
INDUSTRIAL ESTATE
Rec. Grd
Golf Driving Range
Football Ground
Recreation Ground
Darland Banks Public Open Space
Darland Hill
The Wagon at Hale PH
Lake
CAPSTONE FARM COUNTRY PARK
Alpine Ski Centre
Refuse Tip
Whites Woods
Drowhill Woods
North Dane Wood
Sharsted Farm
Kingfisher C.P. School
Shopping Centre
Medical Centre
Sports
LUTON HIGH STREET
CAPSTONE ROAD
ASH TREE LANE
CAPSTONE ROAD
PEAR TREE LANE
NORTH DANE WAY
SHAWSTEAD ROAD
LORDS WOOD LANE
PRINCES AVENUE
WAYFIELD ROAD
KINGSWAY
HUNTERS WAY
ROWLAND AVENUE
LEYTON AVENUE
ALLISON AVENUE
HERITAGE ROAD
CRESTWAY
DOWNSVIEW
FALLOWFIELD
RYDE CLOSE
SHANKLIN CL
VENTNOR CL
HOPEWELL DRIVE
GLENWOOD CLOSE
WILTSHIRE WAY
SOMERSET CLOSE
BERKSHIRE CL
DEVON CLOSE
HAMPSHIRE CL
KINGFISHER DRIVE
WORDSWORTH CL
SHERIDAN CL
HERON AVENUE
WHEATEAR WAY
REDWING CL
THRUSH CL
SPITFIRE CLO
HALIFAX CL
DEFIANT CL
SWIFT CRESCENT
BARLEYMOW CLOSE
RYEGRASS CL
CHARLOTTE CL
CHRISTIE RD
HARDY CL
VIXEN CL
COOK CL
ALLEN CL
JUDKINS CL
HOLDER CL
STANLEY CL
ARCHER RD
STAG ROAD
BOWMAN CL
POACHER CL
TYNE CL
WEY CL
TRENT ROAD
SEVERN RD
TAY CL
FOWEY CL
KINGSTON CRESCENT
CAMDEN CL
RED BRIDGE CL
MERTON CL
GREENWICH CL
WEYBRIDGE CL
RICHMOND CL
LAMBETH CL
EALING CL
SHEPPERTON CL
BROMLEY CL
SCOTBY AVENUE
WETHERAL DR
CHARLES DRIVE
BROADLANDS DR
ROMNEY ROAD
LYDO RD
BURMARSH CL
WITTERSHAM CL
WINCHELSEA RD
ALDINGTON CL
BRENZETT CL
LIMETREE CL
BRAMBLE
HAZEL GROVE
CAMERON CL
BANKSIDE
WALNUT CL
HEATHFIELD CL
SOLENT GDNS
CARLTON CRES
ROWAN LEA
STONECROSS LEA
BRACKEN LEA
MILL LANE
SETTINGTON AV
DURRELL GDNS
THIRD AV
SECOND AV
FIRST AV
PHEASANT RD
ALEXANDRA RD
ALBANY ROAD
NELSON CT
NELSON TER
BEACON RD
KINGS RD
QUEENS RD
HAMILTON TER
HUNTERS WAY WEST
DERBY CL
MONTROSE
PRESTON AV
WINDY RIDGE
AUDLEY AVENUE
YEOMAN

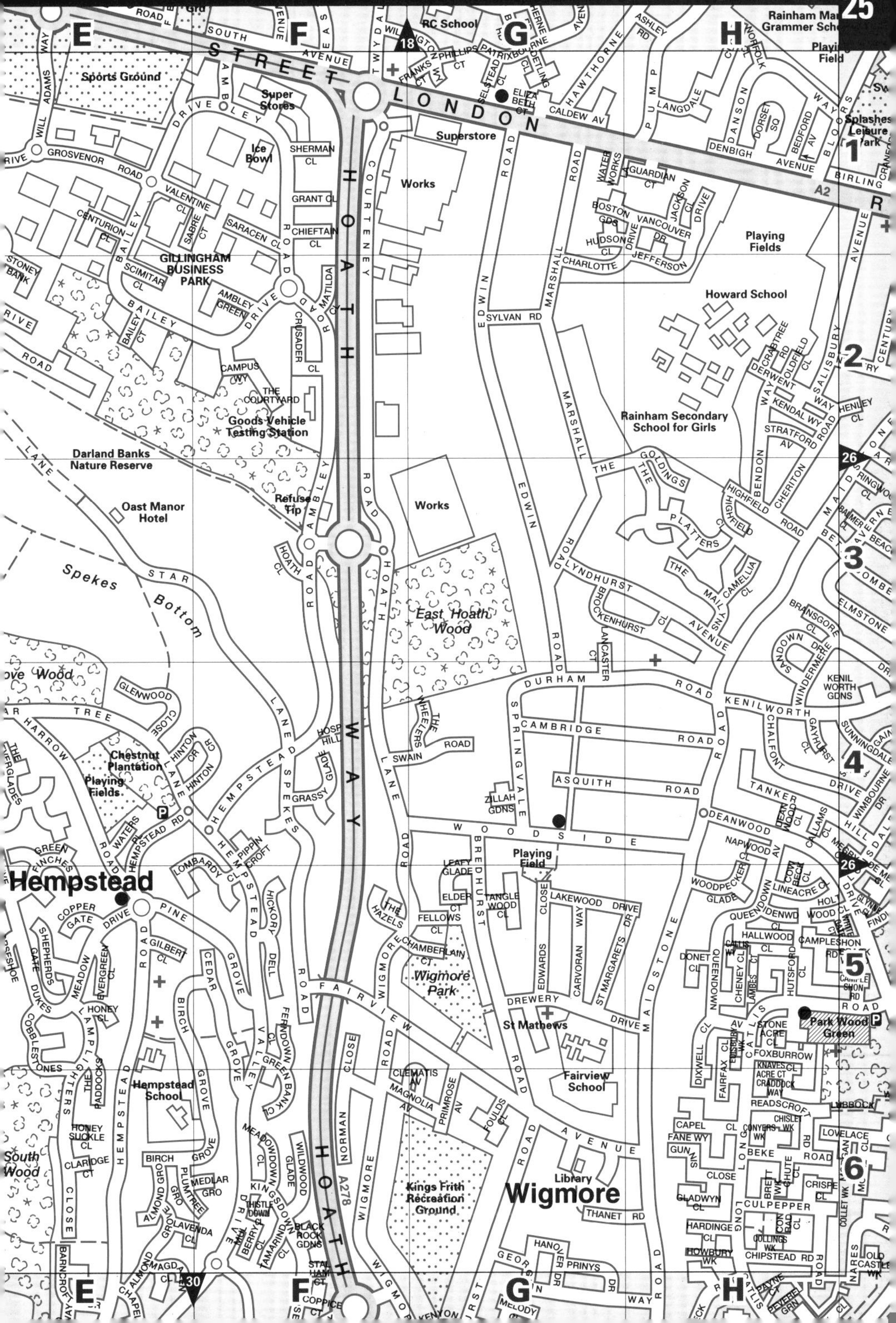
E
F
G
H
1
2
3
4
5
6
18
26
26
30
LONDON STREET
A2
RC School
Rainham Mark Grammer School
Playing Field
Splashes Leisure Park
Sports Ground
Super Stores
Superstore
Ice Bowl
Works
GILLINGHAM BUSINESS PARK
Playing Fields
Howard School
Rainham Secondary School for Girls
Goods Vehicle Testing Station
Darland Banks Nature Reserve
Oast Manor Hotel
Refuse Tip
Works
Spekes Bottom
East Hoath Wood
Chestnut Plantation
Playing Fields
Hempstead
Playing Field
Wigmore Park
St Mathews
Fairview School
Hempstead School
Kings Frith Recreation Ground
Library
Wigmore
Park Wood Green
South Wood
HOATH WAY
A278
GROSVENOR ROAD
VALENTINE CL
CENTURION CL
SABRE CT
SARACEN CL
SCIMITAR CL
BAILEY DRIVE
AMBLEY ROAD
AMBLEY GREEN
SHERMAN CL
GRANT CL
CHIEFTAIN CL
CRUSADER CL
MATILDA CL
CAMPUS WY
THE COURTYARD
COURTENEY ROAD
EDWIN ROAD
MARSHALL ROAD
SYLVAN RD
PUMP LANE
HAWTHORNE
CALDEW AV
LANGDALE
DANSON
DORSET SQ
DENBIGH AVENUE
BEDFORD AV
BLOORS LANE
BIRLING
WATERWORKS ROAD
GUARDIAN CT
BOSTON GDS
VANCOUVER DR
HUDSON CL
JACKSON DRIVE
JEFFERSON
CHARLOTTE
SALISBURY AVENUE
CRABTREE RD
OLDFIELD CL
DERWENT WAY
KENDAL WY
HENLEY CL
STRATFORD AV
BENDON WAY
CHERITON ROAD
HIGHFIELD ROAD
THE GOLDINGS
PLATTERS CL
THE MAIL
CAMELLIA CL
LYNDHURST AVENUE
BROCKENHURST CL
LANCASTER CT
DURHAM ROAD
KENILWORTH DRIVE
KENILWORTH GDNS
SANDOWN DR
WINDERMERE
BRANSGORE CL
ELMSTONE
CAMBRIDGE ROAD
ASQUITH ROAD
SPRINGVALE
ZILLAH GDNS
WOODSIDE
DEANWOOD DRIVE
NAPWOOD AV
WOODPECKER GLADE
TANKER HILL
CHALFONT DRIVE
GAYHURST
SUNNINGDALE
WIMBOURNE DR
STAR LANE
GLENWOOD CLOSE
HINTON CR
HARROW
TREE
HEMPSTEAD LANE
SPEKES ROAD
GRASSY GLADE
HOSP HILL
THE WHEELERS
SWAIN ROAD
WATERS PL
HEMPSTEAD RD
PIPPIN CROFT
LOMBARDY CL
HICKORY DELL
GREEN FINCHES
COPPER GATE
PINE GROVE
GILBERT CL
SHEPHERDS GATE
MEADOW
EVERGREEN CL
HONEY CL
DUKES MEADOW
COBBLESTONES
LAMPLIGHTERS
THE PADDOCKS
HONEYSUCKLE CL
CLARIDGE CT
CEDAR GROVE
BIRCH GROVE
VALLEY
GREEN BANK CL
FERNDOWN
MEADOWDOWN CL
KINGSDOWN
WILDWOOD GLADE
THISTLEDOWN
BERRY
BLACK ROCK GDNS
TAMARIND
ALMOND GRO
PLUMTREE GRO
MEDLAR GRO
LAVENDA
MAGDALEN
BARNCROFT
CHAPEL
STALHAM CT
COPPICE
THE HAZELS
CHAMBERLAIN CT
FAIRVIEW AVENUE
CLEMATIS AV
MAGNOLIA AV
PRIMROSE AV
FOULDS CL
NORMAN CLOSE
WIGMORE ROAD
LEAFY GLADE
ELDER CT
FELLOWS CL
BREDHURST ROAD
TANGLE WOOD CL
LAKEWOOD DRIVE
CARVORAN WAY
ST MARGARETS DR
EDWARDS CLOSE
DREWERY DRIVE
MAIDSTONE ROAD
THANET RD
HANOVER DR
PRINYS DR
GEORGIAN WAY
MELODY
KENYON
QUEENDOWN AV
LINEACRE CL
HOLTWOOD CL
CAMPLESHON RD
HALLWOOD CL
DONET CL
CHENEY CL
HUTSFORD CL
STONEACRE CL
FOXBURROW CL
KNAVES ACRE CT
CRADDOCK WAY
DIXWELL CL
FAIRFAX CL
READSCROFT CL
CAPEL CL
FANE WY
GUNNIS CLOSE
CONYERS WK
CHISLET WK
BEKE ROAD
LOVELACE CL
GLADWYN CL
LONG CATLIS
CULPEPPER
BRETT WK
CHUTE CL
CRISPE CL
HARDINGE CL
COLLINGS WK
HOWBURY WK
CHIPSTEAD RD
PAYNE CT
REVERE GRN
NARES
OLD CASTLE WK
LYBBOCK

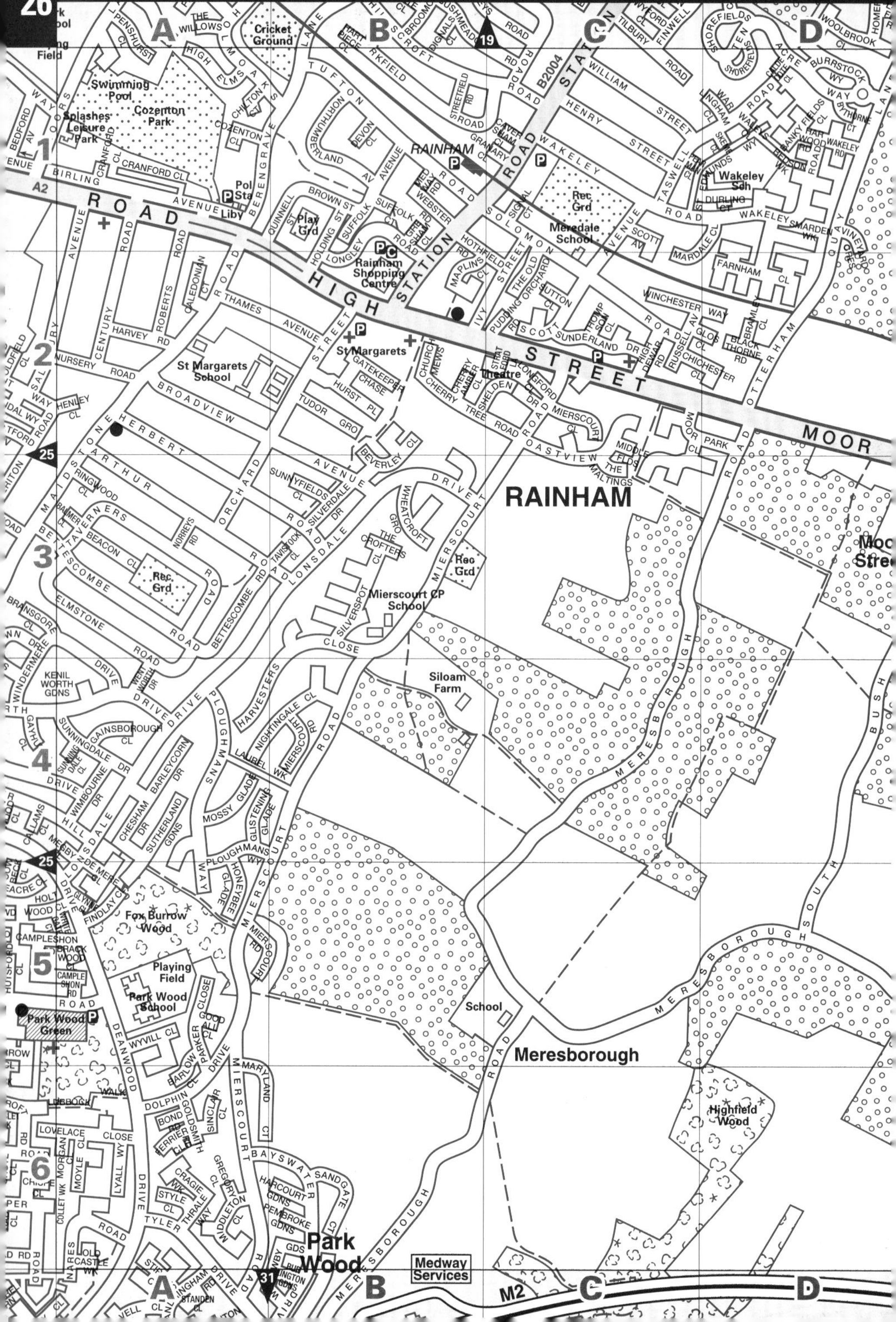
A
B
C
D
1
2
3
4
5
6
19
25
25
31
Cricket Ground
Swimming Pool
Splashes Leisure Park
Cozenton Park
Playing Field
THE WILLOWS
PENSHURST CL
HIGH ELMS
OAKS
CHILTON CT
COZENTON CL
BERENGRAVE
CRANFORD CL
BIRLING
BEDFORD AV
A2
ROAD
AVENUE
Pol Sta
Liby
TUFTON
NORTHUMBERLAND
DEVON CL
HART PIECE CL
BROOMCROFT
DIGNALS CL
BUSHMEADOW
ROAD
STREETFIELD RD
B2004
STATION
ROAD
WILLIAM
STREET
HENRY
STREET
TILBURY
FINWELL
ROAD
SHOREFIELDS
WOOLBROOK CL
BURRSTOCK WY
BYTHORNE CT
RAINHAM
GRANARY
CAVERSHAM CL
WAKELEY
ROAD
SOLOMON
SIGNAL CT
Rec Grd
Meredale School
Wakeley Sch
DURLING CT
SMARDEN WK
VINEYARD CRES
SCOTT AV
MARDALE CL
FARNHAM CL
BROWN ST
QUINNELL ST
HOLDING ST
SUFFOLK
Play Grd
LONGLEY
WEBSTER RD
Rainham Shopping Centre
HIGH
STATION
STREET
MAPLINS CL
HOTHFIELD RD
IVY
THE OLD ORCHARD
PUDDING RD
SUTTON CL
SCOTT
SUNDERLAND DR
WINCHESTER WAY
RUSSELL AV
GLOS CL
CHICHESTER CL
BLACKTHORNE RD
BRAMLEY CL
OTTERHAM
MOOR
CENTURY
HARVEY
ROBERTS RD
CALEDONIAN CT
THAMES AVENUE
NURSERY ROAD
St Margarets School
St Margarets
GATEKEEPER CHASE
HURST PL
TUDOR GRO
BROADVIEW
HERBERT
ARTHUR
RINGWOOD CL
TAVERNERS
BEACON CL
NORREYS RD
ORCHARD
SUNNYFIELDS CL
BEVERLEY CL
AVENUE
SILVERDALE DR
LONSDALE
TAVISTOCK CL
ROAD
DRIVE
WHEATCROFT GRO
THE CROFTERS CL
CHURCH MEWS
CHERRY AMBER CL
STRATFORD
Theatre
LONGFORD
SHELDEN DR
CHERRY TREE ROAD
MIERSCOURT CL
OASTVIEW
THE MALTINGS
MIDDLE FLDS
MOOR PARK CL
ROAD
RAINHAM
MIERSCOURT
Rec Grd
Mierscourt CP School
SILVERSPOT CL
CLOSE
MAIDSTONE
BETTESCOMBE
Rec Grd
BETTESCOMBE RD
ELMSTONE
ROAD
BRANSGORE CL
WINDERMERE
KENILWORTH GDNS
DRIVE
WENTWORTH DR
SUNNINGDALE
GAINSBOROUGH CL
WIMBOURNE DR
HILLSDALE
CHESHAM DR
BARLEYCORN DR
SUTHERLAND GDNS
PLOUGHMANS
HARVESTERS
NIGHTINGALE CL
TURTLE
MIERSCOURT RD
LAUREL WK
MOSSY GLADE
GLISTENING GLADE
PLOUGHMANS WY
HONEYBEE GLADE
WAY
ROAD
Siloam Farm
MERESBOROUGH
SOUTH
BUSH
Moor Street
FINDLAY CL
GLYNNE
Fox Burrow Wood
CAMPLESHON RD
BRACKWOOD
Playing Field
Park Wood School
GOOD ALL CL
CLOSE
PARKER
Park Wood Green
DEANWOOD
WYVILL CL
BARLOW
DRIVE
MIERSCOURT
MARYLAND CT
School
ROAD
Meresborough
MERESBOROUGH
Highfield Wood
DOLPHIN
BOND
FERRIER
GOLDSMITH
SINCLAIR
LOVELACE CLOSE
MORGAN
MOYLE
LYALL WY
CRAGIE WK
STYLE CL
THRALE WAY
GREGORY CL
MIDDLETON CL
BAYSWATER
SANDGATE CT
HARCOURT GDNS
PEMBROKE GDNS
COLLET WK
TYLER DRIVE
ROAD
OLD CASTLE WK
NARES
Park Wood
Medway Services
M2
STANDEN CL
MERESBOROUGH
ROAD

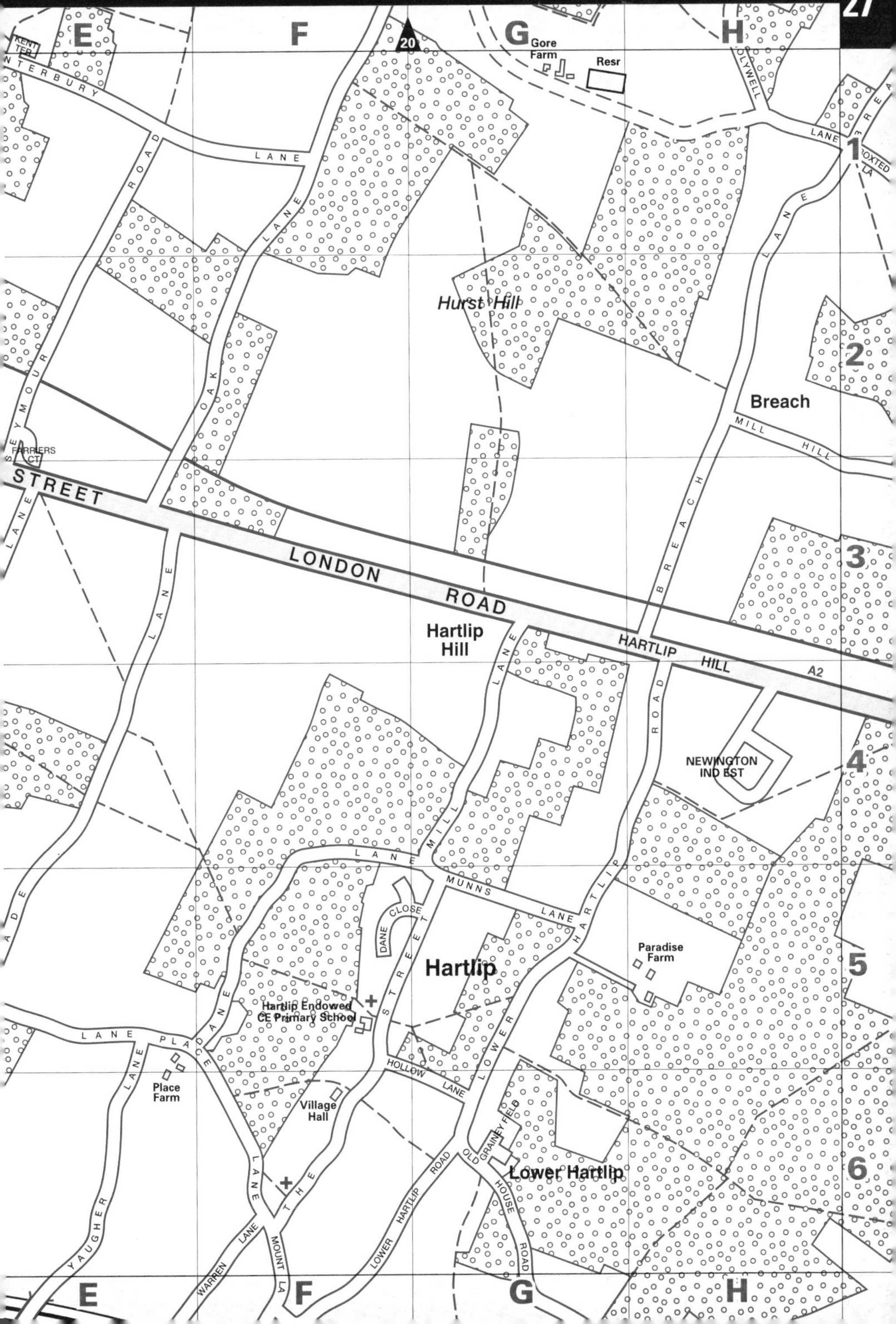
E
F
G
H
Gore Farm
Resr
20
KENT TER
CANTERBURY LANE
HOLYWELL
LANE
ROAD
OAK LANE
Hurst Hill
BREACH LANE
BROXTED LA
1
2
Breach
MILL HILL
SEYMOUR ROAD
FARRIERS CT
STREET
LANE
LONDON ROAD
BREACH ROAD
3
Hartlip Hill
LANE
HARTLIP HILL
A2
ROAD
NEWINGTON IND EST
4
MILL LANE
MUNNS LANE
HARTLIP ROAD
DANE CLOSE
Paradise Farm
Hartlip
5
Hartlip Endowed CE Primary School
STREET
LANE PLACE LANE
Place Farm
HOLLOW LANE
LOWER
GRAINEY FIELD
Village Hall
OLD HOUSE ROAD
Lower Hartlip
6
THE
LANE
YAUGHER LANE
WARREN LANE
MOUNT LA
LOWER HARTLIP ROAD
ROAD
E
F
G
H

A
B
C
D
1
2
3
4
5
6
Syle Wood
Channel Tunnel Rail Link Under Construction
Middle Hill
Bridges Wood
Middlehill Wood
Woolmans Wood Caravan Site (Touring)
Superstore
Bridgewood Manor Hotel
Swimming Pool
BUCKMORE PARK
Buckmore Park Activity Centre
Lord Lees
Blue Bell Hill
Picnic Site
Pits (Disused)
Kit's Coty
Kit's Coty Farm
B2097
ROAD
MAIDSTONE ROAD
CHATHAM ROAD
COMMON ROAD
MILL LANE
THE DOWNS
WARREN ROAD
KINGSWOOD ROAD
SALISBURY ROAD
VINCENT ROAD
BERESFORD ROAD
RUSSELL RD
QUEENSWOOD
COLLINGWOOD RD
OLD CHATHAM RD
A229
VICTORIA CL
KEEFE CL
TODDINGTON CRES
Hall
UPPER ROBIN HOOD LANE
THORN CL
BARLING CL
LAURIE GRAY AV
ROMAN CL
M2 JUNCTION 3
M2
Medway Crematorium
Taddington Wood
TADDINGTON WOOD
PAPION GRO
WALDERSLADE ROAD
HALLSFIELD
SADLERS CL
HOLLAND
AVENUE
CLOSE
WOODHURST
KEMP CL
HURSTWOOD
VALERIAN CL
GEORGE
CAMPION CL
NORTON GRO
KING
CHESTNUT AVENUE
MARSTON CL
WK
HILL FARM CHASE
FARM RD
VICTORIA
OAKLEIGH CL
MONTFORD ROAD
HURST HILL
LOCKSLEY CL
LOWER ROBIN HOOD LANE
FERNBANK CL
FOSTINGTON WAY
Tunbury School
Rec Grd
Hall
CATKIN CLOSE
WOODBURY
FALKLAND PL
WALSHAM RD
TAVISTOCK
SARSEN HTS
HEPPLE WHITE MS
CHIPPENDALE
SHERATON CT
Impton Wood
Rodkin Wood
OAKS DENE
TUNBURY
IMPTON WOODS
Frith Wood
North Downs Way
Hosp (Priv)
Westfield Wood
Walderslade
Playing Field
Lordswood Junior School
WEEDS WOOD
23
LOVE CR
SORRELL
TEASEL
YARROW
MAYWEED
PIMPERNEL WY
SPEEDWELL
SEDGE CRESCENT
ASPEN WY
SILVERWEED
GENTIAN CL
HONEYSUCKLE CL
LARKSPUR RD
JASMINE CL
MALLOW WY
AVENUE
YORK AVENUE
WINCHESTER AV
REPTON WY
ETON CL
RUGBY CL
MANOR GDS
OAKHURST CL
OAK LAND CL
BULRUSH CL
AMANDA CL
KIT HILL AVENUE
TUNBURY AVENUE
NICKLAUS DR
TREVINO DRIVE
MAFEKING ROAD
JACKLIN CL
LONG HURST DR
FORESTERS CL
ROBIN HOOD LANE
WALDERSLADE ROAD
OLLIFFES CL
POLHILL
FRIARS AV
FOREST DRIVE
BOLNER CL
LITTLE JOHN AV
FRENSHAM WALK
VALLEY RISE
COPSE
MARLOW
HAWTHORNS
TUNBURY AV STH
FELDSPAR CL
RODKIN WOOD
P

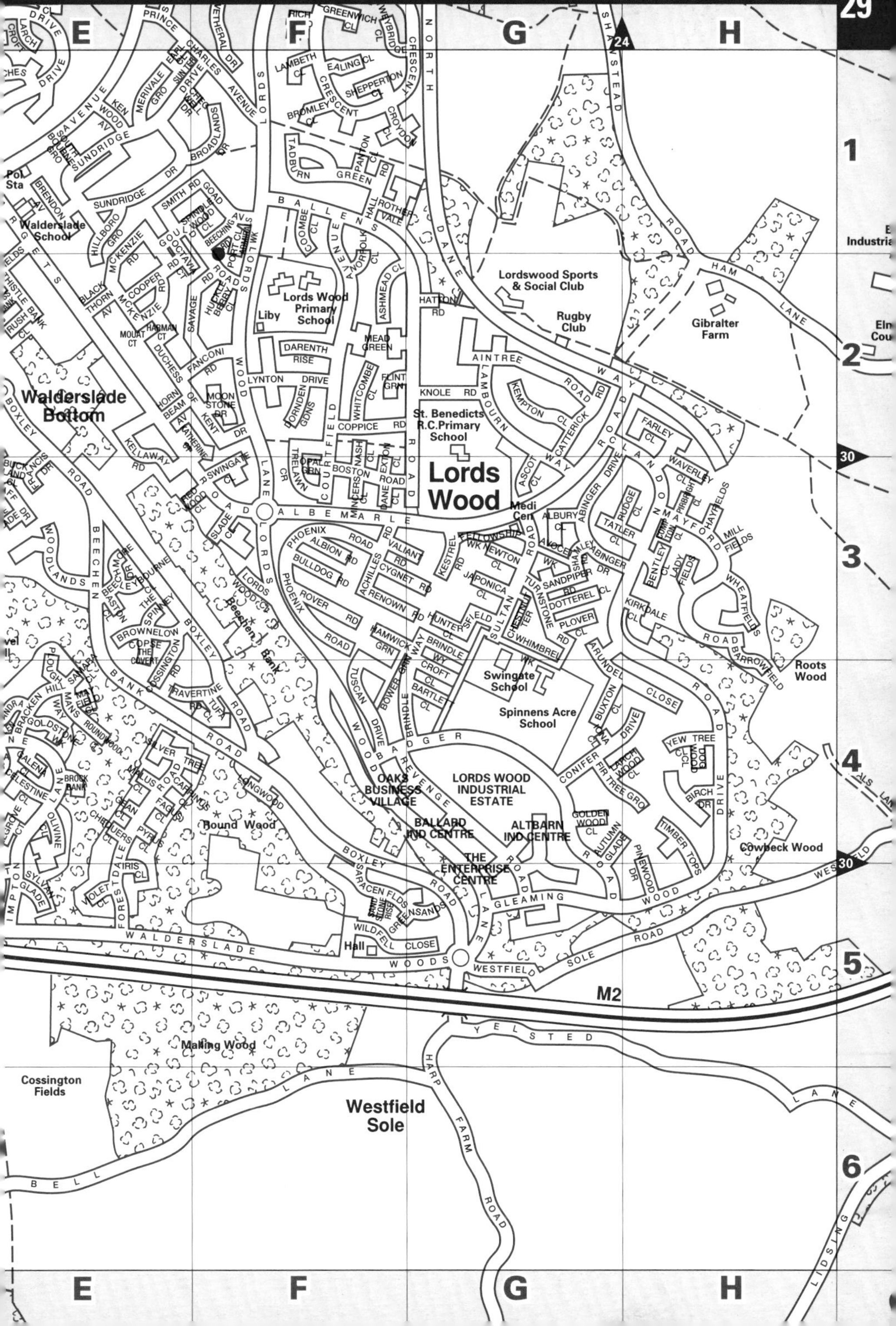
E
F
G
H
1
2
3
4
5
6
24
30
30
Pol Sta
Walderslade School
Walderslade Bottom
Lords Wood Primary School
Liby
Lordswood Sports & Social Club
Rugby Club
Gibralter Farm
St. Benedicts R.C.Primary School
Lords Wood
Medi Cen
Swingate School
Spinnens Acre School
Roots Wood
OAKS BUSINESS VILLAGE
LORDS WOOD INDUSTRIAL ESTATE
BALLARD IND CENTRE
ALTBARN IND CENTRE
THE ENTERPRISE CENTRE
Round Wood
Cowbeck Wood
Beechen Bank
Hall
M2
Malling Wood
Cossington Fields
Westfield Sole
PRINCE CHARLES AVENUE
SUNDRIDGE DR
BROADLANDS DR
LORDS WOOD LANE
NORTH DANE WAY
SHAWSTEAD ROAD
HAM LANE
ALBEMARLE RD
BALLENS RD
BOXLEY ROAD
BEECHEN BANK RD
WALDERSLADE WOODS
WESTFIELD SOLE ROAD
GLEAMING WOOD DR
BADGER RD
REVENGE RD
PHOENIX ROAD
CAPSTONE RD
DARENTH RISE
LYNTON DRIVE
COPPICE RD
AINTREE RD
KNOLE RD
LAMBOURN WAY
KEMPTON CL
CATTERICK RD
ASCOT CL
HATTON RD
ABINGER DRIVE
MAYFORD RD
WHEATFIELDS
BARROWFIELD
ARUNDEL CLOSE
BUXTON CL
YEW TREE CL
BIRCH DR
TIMBER TOPS
PINEWOOD DR
AUTUMN GLADE
GOLDEN WOOD CL
CONIFER DR
FIR TREE GRO
LARCH WOOD
SARACEN FLDS
GREENSANDS
WILDFELL CLOSE
YELSTED RD
HARP FARM ROAD
BELL LANE
LIDSING RD
PLOUGH WENTS

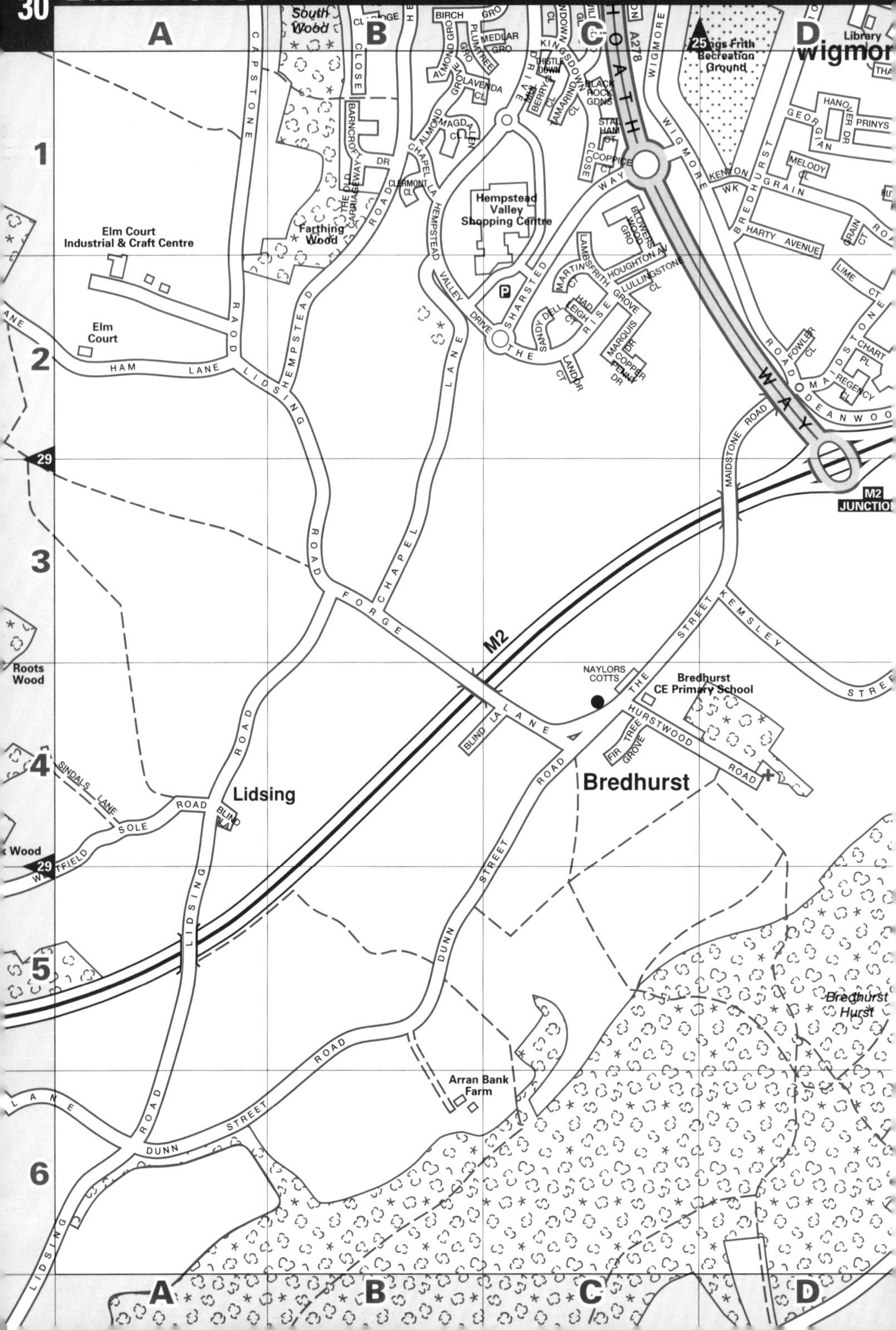
A
B
C
D
1
2
3
4
5
6
South Wood
Farthing Wood
Elm Court Industrial & Craft Centre
Elm Court
Hempstead Valley Shopping Centre
Wigmore
Library
Recreation Ground
M2 JUNCTION
M2
A278
HEMPSTEAD ROAD
CAPSTONE ROAD
HAM LANE
LIDSING ROAD
FORGE LANE
CHAPEL LANE
HEMPSTEAD VALLEY DRIVE
THE STREET
KEMSLEY STREET
MAIDSTONE ROAD
HURSTWOOD ROAD
FIR TREE GROVE
BLIND LA
SOLE ROAD
SINDALS LANE
DUNN STREET
DUNN STREET ROAD
HARTY AVENUE
BREDHURST ROAD
GRAIN ROAD
KENYON WK
WIGMORE ROAD
SHARSTED WAY
THE SANDY DELL
HOUGHTON AV
LULLINGSTONE CL
MARQUIS DR
COPPER PENNY DR
LANDOR CT
HADLEIGH CT
MARTIN CT
BLOWERS WOOD GRO
COPPICE CT
STALHAM CT
BLACK ROCK GDNS
TAMARIND CL
BERRY CL
THISTLE DOWN CL
KINGSDOWN CL
BIRCH GRO
MEDLAR GRO
PLUMTREE GRO
ALMOND GRO
LAVENDA CL
MAGDALEN CL
ALMOND CL
BARNCROFT DR
THE OLD CARRIAGEWAY
CLERMONT CL
CLOSE
CHAPEL LA
GEORGIAN DR
HANOVER DR
PRINYS DR
MELODY CL
LIME CT
FOWLER CL
CHART PL
REGENCY CL
DEANWOOD
GRAIN CT
NAYLORS COTTS
Bredhurst CE Primary School
Bredhurst
Lidsing
Roots Wood
Arran Bank Farm
Bredhurst Hurst
29
25

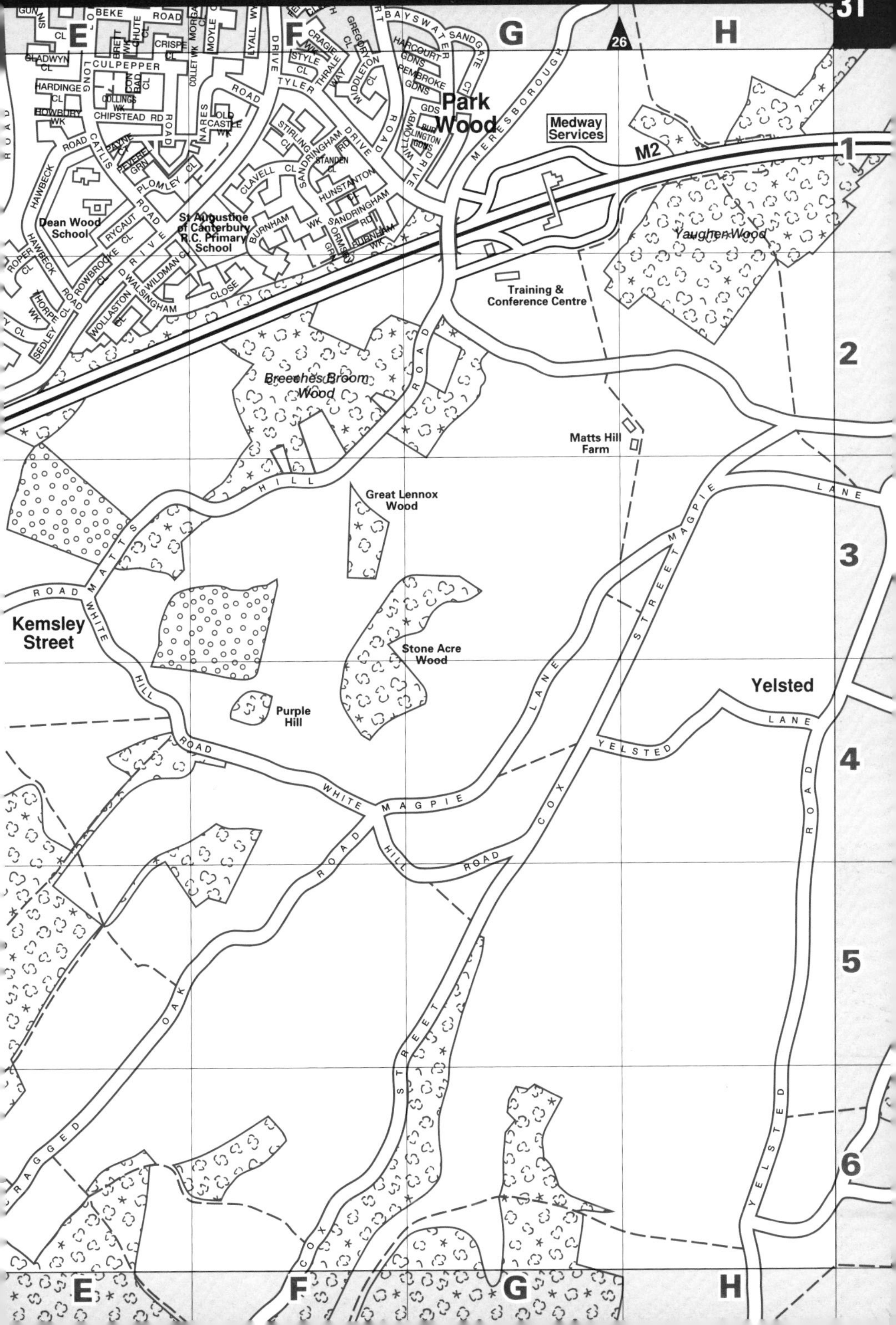
E
F
G
H
26
1
2
3
4
5
6
Park Wood
Medway Services
M2
Yaugher Wood
Training & Conference Centre
Breeches Broom Wood
Matts Hill Farm
Great Lennox Wood
Kemsley Street
Stone Acre Wood
Purple Hill
Yelsted
Dean Wood School
St Augustine of Canterbury R.C. Primary School
BEKE ROAD
CULPEPPER
HARDINGE CL
HOWBURY WK
CHIPSTEAD RD
GLADWYN CL
CRISPE CL
COLLINGS WK
OLD CASTLE WK
TYLER DRIVE
STIRLING CL
SANDRINGHAM DRIVE
STANDEN CL
HUNSTANTON CL
CLAVELL CL
BURNHAM WK
BAYSWATER
SANDGATE CT
HARCOURT GDNS
PEMBROKE GDNS
WILLOWBY GDS
MIDDLETON CL
MERESBOROUGH
PLOMLEY CL
PEVEREL GRN
PAYNE CT
RYCAUT CL
ROWBROOKE CL
WILDMAN CL
WALSINGHAM CLOSE
WOLLASTON CL
HAWBECK ROAD
ROPER CL
THORPE WK
SEDLEY CL
MATTS HILL ROAD
WHITE ROAD
WHITE HILL ROAD
WHITE MAGPIE LANE
YELSTED LANE
YELSTED ROAD
LANE
MAGPIE STREET
COX STREET
HILL ROAD
OAK ROAD
RAGGED
E
F
G
H

A - Z INDEX TO STREETS

with Postcodes

The Index includes some names for which there is insufficient space on the maps. These names are indicated by an * and are followed by the nearest adjoining thoroughfare.

Abbey Rd, Frindsbury ME2 11 F5
Abbey Rd, Twydall ME8 18 B5
Abbots Court Rd ME3 9 G5
Abbotts Cl ME1 15 H5
Abigail Cres ME5 28 D4
Abinger Dr ME5 29 G3
Absolam Ct ME8 18 D6
Academy Dr ME7 25 E1
Achilles Rd ME5 29 F3
Acorn Rd ME7 18 A4
Acre Cl ME1 23 E1
Adelaide Rd ME7 17 G4
Admirals Walk, Lords Wood ME5 29 F1
Admirals Walk, Rochester ME4 16 D1
Admiralty Rd ME2 12 D4
Admiralty Ter, Brompton ME7 17 E1
Admiralty Ter, Upper Upnor ME2 12 D4
Afghan Rd ME4 3 A3
Aintree Rd ME5 29 G2
Ajax Rd ME1 22 D3
Alamein Av ME5 23 G4
Albany Rd, Gillingham ME7 17 H4
Albany Rd, Luton ME4 17 F6
Albany Rd, Rochester ME1 16 A4
Albany Ter, Chatham ME4 3 A3
Albany Ter, Gillingham ME7 17 H3
Albatross Av ME2 14 C1
Albemarle Rd ME5 29 F3
Albert Pl ME2 11 H6
Albert Rd, Chatham ME4 16 D4
Albert Rd, Gillingham ME7 17 F4
Albert Rd, Rochester ME1 16 A4
Albion Rd ME5 29 F3
Albury Cl ME5 29 G3
Aldershot Rd ME5 23 G3
Aldington Cl ME5 24 A6
Alexandra Av ME7 17 H4
Alexandra Glen ME5 29 E4
Alexandra Rd ME4 17 F6
Alfred Cl ME4 17 F6
All Saints Rd ME3 4 B3
Allen Cl ME5 24 A5
Allens Hill ME3 6 A1
Allhallows Rd ME3 5 C4
Allington Dr ME2 11 E5
Allington Rd ME8 18 C4
Allison Av ME7 24 D1
Alma Pl ME2 15 G1
Almon Pl ME1 3 C6
Almond Gro ME7 25 E6
Amanda Cl ME5 28 C1
Ambley Grn ME8 25 F2
Ambley Rd ME8 25 F3
Ambrose Hill ME5 17 G6
Amethyst Av ME5 23 F4
Amherst Hill ME7 16 D2
Amherst Rd ME1 16 B5
Amherst Redoubt ME7 17 E2
Anchor Rd ME1 22 D1
Anchor Wharf ME4 16 D2
Anchorage Cl ME3 5 C5
Anglesey Cl ME5 23 H3
Ansell Av ME4 23 H1
Anson Cl ME5 24 A4
Anthonys Way ME2 12 B4
Appleby Cl ME1 23 E3
Applecross Cl ME1 15 H4
Appledore Rd ME8 18 C4
Archer Rd ME5 24 A5
Archery Cl ME3 7 F2
Arden St ME7 17 F2
Arethusa Rd ME1 22 D2
Argyle Cl ME1 23 F3
Armada Way ME4 16 D5
Armytage Cl ME3 9 G5
Arnhem Dr ME5 23 G4
Arnolde Cl ME2 16 C1
Arran Grn ME2 14 D1
Arthur Rd, Rainham ME8 26 A2
Arthur Rd, Rochester ME1 16 B5
Arundel Cl ME5 29 G3
Ascot Cl ME5 29 G3
Ash Cl, Luton ME5 24 B2
Ash Cl, Twydall ME8 18 C5
Ash Cres ME3 10 C2
Ash Rd ME2 15 F2
Ash Tree La ME5 24 C1
Ashby Cl ME2 6 C5
Ashenden Cl ME2 12 A4
Ashley Rd ME8 19 E6
Ashmead Cl ME5 29 F2
Ashwood Cl ME3 7 F2
Aspen Way ME5 28 C1
Asquith Rd ME8 25 G4
Association Walk ME1 22 D3
Aston Cl ME5 29 E3
Athelstan Rd ME4 16 C6
Atlanta Ct ME4 16 B4
Audley Av ME7 24 D1
Austin Cl ME5 17 H6
Autumn Glade ME5 29 G4
Aveling Cl ME3 9 E4
Aveling Ct*, North St ME2 11 H6
Avery Cl ME3 4 C2
Avery Way ME3 4 B3
Avocet Walk ME5 29 G3
Avondale Rd ME7 17 H2
Aylesford Cres ME8 18 C4

Backfields ME1 15 H3
Baden Rd ME7 17 H1
Bader Cres ME5 23 H3
Badger Rd ME5 29 F4
Baffin Cl ME4 16 D6
Bailey Ct ME8 25 E2
Bailey Dr ME8 25 E2
Bakenham Ho*, The Fairway ME1 22 D1
Baker St ME1 16 A4
Bakers Walk ME1 3 B5
Balfour Rd, Chatham ME4 16 C6
Balfour Rd, Hoo St Werburgh ME3 9 G3
Ballens Rd ME5 29 F1
Balls Cotts ME3 8 B5
Balmer Cl ME8 26 A3
Balmoral Rd ME7 17 G2
Bangor Rd ME2 14 D2
Bank St ME4 17 E5
Banks Rd ME2 11 H5
Bankside ME5 24 A2
Banky Fields Cl ME8 26 D1
Banning St ME2 11 H5
Barberry Av ME5 23 E6
Bardell Ter ME1 3 D6
Barfleur Manor*, Middle St ME7 17 E1
Barkis Cl ME1 23 E3
Barleycorn Dr ME8 26 A4
Barleymow Cl ME5 24 A4
Barling Cl ME5 28 A4
Barlow Cl ME8 26 A6
Barnaby Ter ME1 16 A6
Barnard Ct ME4 16 D6
Barncroft Dr ME7 30 B1
Barnfield ME5 23 H2
Barnsole Rd ME7 17 H3
Barnwood Cl ME1 22 C2
Baron Cl ME7 18 A1
Barrier Rd ME4 16 D3
Barrington Cl ME5 23 G5
Barrowfield ME5 29 H3
Bartlett Cl ME5 29 G4
Barton Rd ME2 11 G6
Basi Cl ME2 12 A5
Batchelor St ME4 3 C2
Bath Hard La ME1 16 B3
Battlesmere Rd ME3 7 F1
Bayswater Dr ME8 26 A6
Beacon Cl ME8 26 A3
Beacon Hill ME5 17 G6
Beacon Hill La ME3 8 B6
Beacon Rd ME5 17 F5
Beaconsfield Av ME7 17 H3
Beaconsfield Rd ME4 16 D5
Bearsted Cl ME8 18 C4
Beatty Av ME7 18 B4
Beatty Rd ME1 23 E2
Beaufort Ct ME2 16 C2
Beaufort Rd ME2 11 E5
Beaulieu Rise ME1 16 B6
Bedford Av ME8 25 H1
Bedgebury Cl ME1 23 E2
Bedson Walk ME8 26 D1
Bedwin Cl ME1 23 E3
Beech Gro ME3 10 C2
Beech Rd ME2 15 F2
Beechen Bank Rd ME5 29 E3
Beeching Rd ME5 29 F1
Beechings Grn ME8 19 E5
Beechings Way ME8 18 B4
Beechmore Dr ME5 29 E3
Beechwood Av ME5 17 H6
Begonia Av ME8 18 D5
Beke Rd ME8 25 H6
Bell La ME14 29 E6
Bellgrove Ct ME5 29 E4
Bells La ME3 9 F2
Belmont Rd ME7 17 F3
Bendon Way ME8 25 H3
Benedict Cl ME2 6 D5
Benenden Rd ME2 12 A4
Bentley Cl ME5 29 H3
Berber Rd ME2 11 H5
Berengrave La ME8 19 G5
Beresford Av ME1 16 C6
Beresford Rd, Gillingham ME7 17 H3
Beresford Rd, Kit's Coty ME20 28 A6
Bergland Pk ME2 12 B5
Berkeley Cl ME1 23 E2
Berkshire Cl ME5 24 B3
Bessies La ME3 5 C1
Best St ME4 3 B2
Bettescombe Rd ME8 26 A3
Beverley Cl ME8 26 B2
Bill Street Rd ME2 12 A4
Bilsington Cl ME5 24 A5
Bingham Rd ME2 12 A4
Bingley Rd ME1 16 B3
Binland Gro ME5 23 E5
Binnacle Rd ME1 22 D2
Binney Rd ME3 4 B3
Birch Dr ME5 29 H4
Birch Gro ME7 25 E6
Birchfields ME5 29 E2
Birkhall Cl ME5 23 H5
Birling Av ME8 25 H1
Bishop La ME9 20 D5
Bishops Walk ME1 3 C6
Bishopsbourne Grn ME8 18 D4
Black Rock Gdns ME7 25 F6
Blackman Cl ME3 9 F3
Blackthorn Av ME5 29 E2
Blackthorne Rd ME8 26 D2
Blaker Av ME1 23 F2
Bleakwood Rd ME5 23 G6
Blean Rd ME8 18 D6
Blenheim Av ME4 16 B6
Bligh Way ME2 14 C1
Blind La ME7 30 B4
Blockmakers Ct ME4 17 E6
Bloors La ME8 25 H1
Bloors Wharf Rd ME8 19 G4
Blowers Wood Gro ME7 30 C1
Blue Boar La ME1 3 C5
Bluebell Cl ME7 18 A2
Bodiam Cl ME8 18 D5
Boley Hill ME1 3 B5
Bolner Cl ME5 28 D3
Bond Rd ME8 26 A6
Bonnington Grn ME8 19 E5
Booth Rd ME4 16 D5
Bootham Cl ME2 15 E3
Borough Rd ME7 17 G4
Borstal Mews ME1 15 G6
Borstal Rd ME1 15 H5
Borstal St ME1 15 G6
Boston Gdns ME8 25 G1
Boston Rd ME5 29 F3
Boughton Cl ME8 18 D5
Boundary Rd ME4 3 A3
Bournville Av ME4 23 F1
Bower Grn ME5 29 F4
Bowes Rd ME2 11 H6
Bowesden La ME3 10 A5
Bowman Cl ME5 24 A5
Boxley Rd ME5 29 E2
Brabourne Av ME8 18 D4
Bracken Hill ME5 29 E4
Bracken Lea ME5 24 A1
Brackwood Cl ME8 26 A5
Bradfields Av ME5 23 G5
Bradfields Av West ME5 23 G5
Bradfords Cl ME4 13 F3
Bradley Rd ME2 6 A5
Bradshaw Cl ME9 20 D5
Brake Av ME5 23 F6
Brambledown ME5 24 A2
Brambletree Cres ME1 15 F5
Bramley Cl ME8 26 D2
Bramley Rise ME2 11 E5
Bransgore Cl ME8 25 H3
Brasenose Av ME7 17 H4
Brasted Ct ME2 11 G4
Breach La ME9
Bredgar Rd ME8
Bredhurst Rd ME8
Brenchley Cl ME1
Brenchley Rd ME8
Brendon Av ME5
Brent Cl ME5
Brenzett Cl ME5
Breton Rd ME1
Brett Walk ME8
Brewer Rd ME3
Briar Dale ME3
Brice Rd ME3
Brick Field Vw ME2
Bridge Rd, Chatham ME7
Bridge Rd, Rochester ME1
Brier Cl ME5
Bright Rd ME4
Brindle Way ME5
Brisbane Rd ME4
Brissenden Cl ME2
Bristol Cl ME2
Britannia Cl ME2
Britannia Rd ME3
Britton St ME7
Broadlands Dr ME5
Broadview Av ME8
Broadway ME8
Broadwood Rd ME3
Brock Bank ME5
Brockenhurst Cl ME8
Bromley Cl ME5
Brompton Cl ME4
Brompton Farm Rd ME2
Brompton Hill ME4
Brompton La ME2
Brompton Rd ME7
Bronington Cl ME5
Brook La ME3
Brooklyn Paddock ME7
Brookmead Rd ME3
Brookside ME3
Broom Hill Rd ME2
Broomcroft Rd ME8
Brown St ME8
Browndens Rd ME2
Brownelow Copse ME5
Brownhill Cl ME5
Bryant Rd ME2
Bryant St ME4
Buckingham Rd ME7
Buckland Cl ME5
Buckland Rd ME3
Bull La, Lower Highan ME3
Bull La, Rochester ME1
Bulldog Rd ME5
Buller Rd ME4
Bulrush Cl ME5
Bumbles Cl ME1
Bunters Hill Rd ME3
Burgess Rd ME2
Burham Rd ME1
Burleigh Cl ME2
Burlington Gdns ME8
Burma Way ME5
Burmarsh Cl ME5
Burnham Walk ME8
Burns Rd ME7
Burnt House Cl ME2
Burnt Oak Ter ME7
Burntwick Dr ME9
Burritt Mews ME1

ritt St ME1 16 A4
rows La ME3 5 C6
rstock Way ME8 20 A6
ton Cl ME3 12 A2
sh Rd ME2 14 A5
shmeadow Rd ME8 19 G6
t Haw Cl ME3 9 G5
termere Cl ME7 18 B2
ton Dr ME3 5 C4
tway La ME3 6 A1
xton Cl ME5 29 G4
ron Rd ME7 17 F4
thorne Ct ME8 26 D1

dnam Cl ME2 11 E6
gney Cl ME2 12 A3
ldecote Cl ME8 20 A6
ldew Av ME8 18 D6
edonian Ct ME8 26 A2
llams Cl ME8 25 H4
llis Way ME8 25 H5
mbria Av ME1 15 F6
mbridge Rd,
Rainham ME8 25 G4
mbridge Rd,
Strood ME2 11 G5
mbridge Ter ME4 3 B2
mden Cl ME5 24 A6
mden Rd ME7 13 H6
mellia Cl ME8 25 H3
meron Cl ME5 24 A2
mpion Cl ME5 28 C1
mpleshon Rd ME8 25 H5
mpus Way ME8 25 F2
nadian Av ME7 18 A3
nal Rd ME2 15 H1
non Cl ME1 15 H5
nterbury La ME8 20 B6
nterbury St ME7 17 G4
pel Cl ME8 25 H6
pstone Rd ME5 24 B1
rdens Rd ME3 7 F2
rdigan Cl ME3 5 B2
risbrooke Rd ME2 11 E4
rlisle Cl ME2 14 D2
rlton Av ME7 17 H4
rlton Cres ME5 24 B2
rnation Rd ME2 10 D6
rpeaux Cl ME4 3 D3
rpenters Cl ME1 16 B6
rpinus Cl ME5 29 E4
rrington Cl ME7 18 A2
rton Cl ME1 16 B5
rton Rd ME3 10 B2
rvoran Way ME8 25 G5
stle Av ME1 16 A4
stle Hill ME1 3 B4
stle Rd ME4 17 E6
stle St ME2 12 C4
stle View Mews ME1 3 B4
stle View Rd ME2 11 G6
stlemaine Av ME7 18 A2
therine St ME1 16 B5
tkin Cl ME5 28 C4
tterick Rd ME5 29 G2
vell Cl ME8 31 F1
vendish Av ME7 17 H2
vendish Rd ME1 16 B5
versham Cl ME8 26 C1
cil Av, Rainham ME8 18 C6
cil Av, Strood ME2 11 H5
cil Rd ME1 16 A4
dar Gro ME7 25 F5
dar Rd ME2 15 E2
estine Cl ME5 29 E4
metery Rd ME2 6 C5
ntral Av ME4 13 E6
ntral Parade ME1 16 A6
ntral Park Gdns ME4 16 B5
ntral Rd ME2 11 G6

Centurion Cl ME8 25 E1
Century Rd ME8 26 A2
Chada Av ME7 17 H5
Chaffes La ME9 20 D6
Chaffes Ter ME9 20 D5
Chaffinch Cl ME5 23 H4
Chalfont Dr ME8 25 H4
Chalgrove Mews ME2 6 C5
Chalk Pitt Hill ME4 16 D5
Chalkenden Av ME8 18 B5
Chalky Bank Rd ME8 19 G5
Chamberlain Ct ME8 25 G5
Chamberlain Rd ME4 17 F5
Chancery Rd ME3 6 C2
Chapel Ct ME3 4 C5
Chapel La,
Hempstead ME7 30 B1
Chapel La,
Upper Halling ME2 6 A5
Chapel Rd ME3 4 C5
Chaplin Cl ME3 12 A2
Chapter Rd ME2 11 F6
Charing Rd ME8 18 D5
Chariot Way ME2 15 E4
Charles Dickens Av ME3 10 C3
Charles Dr ME2 14 B5
Charles St,
Chatham ME4 16 C4
Charles St,
Strood ME2 15 G1
Charlotte Cl ME5 24 A4
Charlotte Dr ME8 25 G2
Chart Pl ME8 30 D2
Charter St,
Chatham ME4 16 D6
Charter St,
Gillingham ME7 17 F1
Chartwell Cl ME2 11 H4
Chatham Gro ME4 23 G1
Chatham Hill ME5 17 E4
Chatham Rd ME5,20 28 A4
Chatsworth Dr ME2 11 H4
Chatsworth Rd ME7 17 G1
Chattenden La ME3 8 B5
Chaucer Cl ME2 12 C6
Chaucer Rd ME7 17 G5
Chegwell Dr ME5 23 H6
Chelmar Rd ME4 17 E4
Chelmsford Rd ME2 14 D2
Cheney Cl ME8 25 H5
Chequers Cl ME5 29 E4
Chequers Ct ME2 11 G4
Cherbourg Cres ME5 23 G3
Cheriton Rd ME8 25 H3
Cherry Amber Cl ME8 26 B2
Cherry Tree Rd ME8 26 B2
Chesham Dr ME8 26 A4
Chester Cl ME2 14 D2
Chester Rd ME7 17 H5
Chesterfield Cl ME8 19 F6
Chesterton Rd ME3 6 B2
Chestnut Av ME5 28 C2
Chestnut Rd ME2 15 E2
Chestnut Ter ME5 29 G3
Chetney Cl ME2 10 C6
Chevening Cl ME5 23 H5
Chicago Av ME7 18 A3
Chichester Cl ME8 26 C2
Chickfield Gdns ME5 17 G6
Chieftain Cl ME8 25 F1
Childscroft Rd ME8 19 G6
Chilham Cl ME4 3 A3
Chilham Rd ME8 18 B5
Chillington Cl ME2 6 A5
Chilliwack Rd ME3 8 A4
Chilton Ct ME8 19 F6
Chilton Dr ME3 10 B2
Chippendale Cl ME5 28 D4
Chipstead Rd ME8 25 H6
Chislet Walk ME8 25 H6

Christchurch Ct*,
High St ME5 24 B1
Christie Cl ME5 24 A4
Christmas La ME3 5 A2
Christmas St ME7 18 A1
Church Cl ME3 6 B1
Church Farm Cl ME3 9 G5
Church Farm Rd ME9 20 D4
Church Grn ME2 12 A5
Church Hill ME5 17 G6
Church Hill Pl ME3 5 A2
Church La ME4 16 D1
Church Mews ME8 26 B2
Church Path,
Lower Halstow ME9 21 G4
Church Path,
Strood ME2 11 H6
Church St,
Chatham ME4 3 C3
Church St, Cliffe ME3 6 B3
Church St,
Gillingham ME7 18 A1
Church St,
Hoo St Werburgh ME3 9 G5
Church St,
Lower Higham ME3 7 A3
Church St,
Rochester ME1 16 A4
Church Ter ME5 17 G6
Churchill Av ME5 23 G5
Churchlands*,
Palmerston Rd ME4 23 G1
Chute Cl ME8 25 H6
Cinnabar Cl ME5 29 E4
City Way ME1 16 B4
Clandon Rd ME5 29 G2
Claremont Way ME4 3 C3
Clarence Av ME1 16 A4
Clarence Rd ME4 17 F6
Clarendon Gdns ME2 11 G5
Claridge Ct ME7 25 E6
Cleave Rd ME7 17 H5
Clematis Av ME8 25 F6
Clermont Cl ME7 30 B1
Cleveland Rd ME7 17 H1
Cliffe Rd ME2 11 G4
Clifton Cl ME2 15 F1
Clifton Rd ME7 17 G1
Clinch St ME3 5 C1
Clinton Av ME2 11 E5
Clipper Cl ME2 16 C1
Clipper Ct ME2 16 C1
Clive Rd ME1 16 A4
Cloisterham Rd ME1 23 E3
Cloudesley Cl ME1 22 C1
Clover Bank Vw ME5 23 H4
Clover Lay ME8 20 A6
Clover St ME4 3 B3
Coachmans Mews ME1 3 C6
Coast Guard Cotts ME3 4 C6
Cobb Cl ME2 11 E5
Cobden Rd ME4 17 F5
Cobdown Gro ME8 19 H5
Cobham Cl ME2 11 E6
Cobham Rise ME7 18 A3
Coblestones ME7 25 E5
Cobtree Cl ME5 24 A2
Colchester Cl ME5 23 G3
Colewood Dr ME2 10 C6
College Av ME7 17 F3
College Rd ME4 13 E6
College Yard ME1 3 B5
Collet Walk ME8 26 A6
Collings Walk ME8 25 H6
Collingwood Rd ME20 28 A6
Collis St ME2 11 G5
Columbine Cl ME2 11 E6
Columbine Rd ME2 15 E1
Commercial Rd ME2 15 H1
Commissioners Rd ME2 12 A5

Common La ME3 6 C1
Common Rd,
Blue Bell Hill ME5 28 A4
Common Rd,
Cliffe Woods ME3 7 F4
Common Wall ME3 6 D1
Compass Cl ME1 22 D1
Compton Cl ME5 29 H3
Concord Av ME5 23 F5
Coney Mews ME4 23 H1
Conifer Dr ME5 29 G4
Coniston Cl ME7 18 B2
Connaught Rd,
Chatham ME4 17 F6
Connaught Rd,
Gillingham ME7 17 G3
Conrad Cl ME8 25 H6
Constitution Hill ME5 17 F5
Constitution Rd ME5 17 F5
Conway Cl ME2 11 E5
Conway Mews ME7 17 E2
Conyers Walk ME8 25 H6
Cooden Cl ME8 19 H6
Cook Cl ME5 24 A4
Cookham Hill ME1 15 G5
Cookham Wood Rd
ME1 22 C3
Cooling Rd, Cliffe ME3 6 B3
Cooling Rd,
High Halstow ME3 5 A2
Cooling Rd,
Strood ME2 11 H3
Cooling St ME3 6 D3
Coombe Cl ME5 29 F1
Coombe Rd ME3 9 F4
Cooper Rd ME5 29 E2
Copenhagen Rd ME7 17 G3
Copperfield Cres ME3 10 C3
Copperfield Rd ME1 16 A6
Coppergate ME7 25 E5
Copperhouse La ME7 18 C2
Copperhouse Rd ME2 10 C6
Copperpenny Dr ME7 30 C2
Coppice Ct ME7 30 C1
Coppice Rd ME5 29 F2
Cordelia Cres ME1 15 G6
Corkwell St ME4 16 C5
Cormorant Cl ME2 14 C1
Cornwall Rd,
Gillingham ME7 17 G1
Cornwall Rd,
Rochester ME1 16 A4
Cornwallis Av,
Chatham ME4 23 F1
Cornwallis Av,
Gillingham ME7 18 B3
Coronation Rd,
Grain ME3 4 C5
Coronation Rd,
Luton ME5 17 G6
Corporation Rd ME7 17 H1
Corporation St ME1 3 B4
Corral Cl ME5 17 H6
Cossack St ME1 16 A4
Cossington Rd ME5 29 E4
Cottage Rd ME4 16 D2
Cottall Av ME4 16 D6
Coulman St ME7 17 H3
Court Lodge Rd ME7 18 A1
Courteney Rd ME8 25 F1
Courtfield Av ME5 29 F3
Coventry Cl ME2 15 E2
Coverdale Cl ME5 23 H3
Cowbeck Cl ME8 25 H5
Cowdrey Cl ME1 15 H6
Cowper Rd ME7 17 G5
Cowstead La ME8 19 F4
Cox St ME14 31 F6
Cozenton Cl ME8 26 A1
Crabtree Rd ME8 25 H2

Craddock Way ME8 25 H6
Cragie Walk ME8 26 A6
Cranbrook Cl ME8 18 D5
Cranford Cl ME8 26 A1
Cranleigh Gdns ME4 16 B5
Cranmere Ct ME2 12 A5
Crescent Way ME5 23 E5
Cressey Ct ME4 3 A3
Crest Rd ME1 16 A6
Crestway ME5 24 A2
Crispe Cl ME8 25 H6
Crispin Rd ME2 11 E5
Croft Cl ME5 29 G4
Cromer Rd ME2 11 H5
Cromwell Ter ME4 17 E5
Crosier Ct ME9 20 D4
Crosley Rd ME7 17 H5
Cross St, Chatham ME4 3 C2
Cross St,
Gillingham ME7 17 G2
Cross St, Strood ME2 11 H5
Cross Ways ME1 16 A5
Crossways ME5 23 F5
Crouch Hill Ct ME9 21 G5
Crow La ME1 3 C6
Crown St ME7 17 G2
Croydon Cl ME5 29 F1
Crundale Rd ME8 18 D5
Crusader Cl ME8 25 F2
Crutches La ME2 10 B5
Cuckolds Green Rd ME3 5 A4
Culpeper Cl ME2 16 B1
Culpepper ME8 25 H6
Culpepper Rd ME8 31 E1
Cumberland Dr ME9 21 G5
Cumberland Rd ME7 13 F6
Cunningham Cres ME5 23 H3
Curlew Av ME9 21 G5
Curlew Cres ME2 14 C1
Curtis Way ME1 23 E3
Curzon Rd ME4 16 D5
Cuxton Rd ME2 15 E4
Cygnet Rd ME5 29 F3
Cypress Ct ME7 18 B2
Cypress Rd ME2 12 A4

Daffodil Rd ME2 11 E6
Dagmar Rd ME4 17 E6
Dale Rd ME1 16 A5
Dale St ME4 16 C6
Dalison Ct ME2 6 D6
Dalton St ME7 17 G2
Damien Cl ME4 17 E6
Dane Cl, Hartlip ME9 27 F5
Dane Cl,
Lords Wood ME5 29 F3
Dane La ME9 27 F5
Danes Hill ME7 18 B1
Danson Way ME8 25 H1
Darby Gdns ME3 10 C2
Darenth Rise ME5 29 F2
Dargets Rd ME5 29 E1
Darland Av ME7 18 A6
Darnley Cl ME2 15 E1
Darnley Rd ME2 15 E2
Dart Cl ME2 15 F1
Dashmonden Cl ME2 12 A3
Davenport Av ME7 17 H1
Dawes St ME7 17 F3
De Mere Cl ME8 26 A5
Deacon Cl ME2 11 F6
Dean Rd ME2 11 F6
Deanwood Cl ME8 25 H4
Deanwood Dr ME8 26 A5
Defiant Cl ME5 24 A4
Defoe Cl ME5 24 A4
Delce Rd ME1 16 B3
Denbigh Av ME8 25 H1
Denison Mews ME3 5 C5
Denton Grn ME8 18 D4

Derby Rd ME5 17 H6
Derwent Way ME8 25 H2
Detling Cl ME8 18 D6
Devon Cl, Rainham ME8 26 B1
Devon Cl, Wayfield ME5 24 B3
Devonshire Rd ME7 17 G1
Dial Cl ME7 18 B1
Dial Rd ME7 18 B2
Dickens Ct, Higham ME3 10 C1
Dickens Ct, Medway City Est ME2 12 B6
Dickens Rd ME1 16 A5
Dickensian Cl ME3 5 A6
Dignals Cl ME8 19 G6
Dillywood La ME3 11 E4
Dixwell Cl ME8 25 H6
Dock Rd ME4 16 D2
Doddington Rd ME8 19 E5
Doggetts Row ME3 4 C5
Doggetts Sq ME2 15 H1
Dogwood Cl ME5 29 H4
Dolphin Dr ME8 26 A6
Dombey Cl, Higham ME3 10 C2
Dombey Cl, Rochester ME1 16 A5
Donet Cl ME8 25 H5
Dongola Rd ME2 11 H5
Dorchester Cl ME3 7 E2
Dornden Gdns ME5 29 F2
Dorrit Way ME1 16 B6
Dorset Sq ME8 25 H1
Dotterel Cl ME5 29 G3
Doust Way ME1 16 B3
Dove Cl ME5 23 H4
Downer Ct ME1 23 F2
Downside ME2 11 G6
Downsview ME5 24 A2
Drakes Av ME2 11 G5
Drakes Cl ME9 20 D5
Drayton Cl ME3 5 B2
Drewery Dr ME8 25 G5
Duchess Cl ME2 11 E5
Duchess of Kent Dr ME5 29 E2
Dukes Meadow Dr ME7 25 E4
Duncan Rd ME7 17 G3
Dunkirk Dr ME5 23 G4
Dunn Street Rd ME14 30 A6
Dunnings La ME1 16 A3
Durham Rd ME8 25 G4
Durling Ct ME8 26 D1
Durrell Gdns ME5 24 A1
Duval Dr ME1 23 F2
Dux Court Rd, High Halstow ME3 5 A3
Dux Court Rd, Hoo St Werburgh ME3 9 E1

Ealing Cl ME5 24 A6
Earl Cl ME5 23 H6
East End Rd ME4 13 G5
East Hill ME5 24 B2
East Rd ME4 12 D6
East Row ME1 3 C6
East St, Chatham ME4 17 E5
East St, Gillingham ME7 17 G2
Eastcourt Grn ME8 18 C4
Eastcourt La ME7,8 18 C6
Eastern Rd ME7 18 B1
Eastgate ME1 3 C6
Eastgate Ct ME1 3 C6
Eastgate Ter ME1 3 C6
Eastling Cl ME8 19 E5
Eden Av ME5 23 G3
Eden Rd ME3 5 A2
Edinburgh Rd, Gillingham ME7 17 G3
Edinburgh Rd, Grain ME3 4 C5
Edinburgh Rd, Luton ME4 17 F6
Edisbury Walk ME8 25 H5
Edward St, Chatham ME4 17 E5
Edward St, Strood ME2 11 H6
Edwards Cl ME8 25 G5
Edwin Rd ME8 25 G3
Egret Cl ME4 13 E4
Elaine Av ME2 15 E1
Elder Ct ME8 25 G5
Eldon St ME4 3 D2
Elford Rd ME3 6 B2
Elgin Gdns ME2 14 D3
Elham Cl ME8 18 D5
Elizabeth Ct ME8 25 G1
Ellison Way ME8 19 H6
Elm Av, Chatham ME4 23 F1
Elm Av, Chattenden ME3 8 C5
Elm Cl ME3 10 C2
Elm Rd ME7 18 A2
Elm Tree Dr ME1 15 G6
Elmfield ME8 18 B5
Elmhurst Gdns ME4 16 B5
Elmstone Rd ME8 26 A3
Elmwood Rd ME3 8 A4
Ely Cl ME8 19 F5
Embassy Cl ME7 24 D2
Emerald Cl ME1 23 E3
Emily Rd ME5 24 A5
Englefield Cres ME3 7 F2
Enterprise Cl ME2 12 B5
Ernest Rd ME4 17 E5
Esplanade ME1 3 A6
Essex Rd ME2 6 C4
Estelle Cl ME1 23 E3
Ethelbert Rd ME1 16 A4
Eton Cl ME5 28 D1
Eva Rd ME7 17 G5
Evelyn Cl ME2 12 A5
Everest Dr ME3 9 F5
Everest La ME2 11 H5
Everest Mews ME3 9 G5
Evergreen Cl, Hempstead ME7 25 E5
Evergreen Cl, Higham ME3 10 B2
Ewart Rd ME4 23 F1
Exeter Walk ME1 22 D3
Exmouth Rd ME7 13 G6
Exton Cl ME5 29 F3

Factory Farm La ME1 15 F6
Fagus Cl ME5 29 E4
Fairfax Cl ME8 25 H6
Fairlead Rd ME1 23 E1
Fairview Av ME8 25 F5
Fairview Dr ME3 10 C1
Fairway Cl ME1 22 D1
Falkland Pl ME5 28 C4
Fallowfield ME5 24 A2
Fanconi Rd ME5 29 F2
Fane Way ME8 25 H6
Farley Cl ME5 29 H2
Farm Hill Av ME2 11 F4
Farm Rd ME5 28 C2
Farmdale Av ME1 15 F5
Farnham Cl ME8 26 D2
Farraday Cl ME1 23 E2
Farriers Ct ME8 27 E2
Featherby Rd ME8 18 B6
Feldspar Cl ME5 28 D4
Fellows Cl ME8 25 G5
Fennel Cl ME1 15 G4
Fernbank Cl ME5 28 C3
Ferndale Rd ME7 17 H2
Ferndown Cl ME7 25 F5
Ferrier Cl ME8 26 A6
Ferry Rd ME2 6 D5
Field Cl ME5 23 F5
Fieldworks Rd ME4 13 E6
Findlay Cl ME8 26 A5
Finwell Rd ME8 19 H6
Fir Tree Gro ME5 29 G4
Firethorne Cl ME7 18 A2
First Av, Chatham ME4 17 G6
First Av, Gillingham ME7 18 A5
Firtree Gro ME7 30 C4
Fisher Rd ME5 23 H3
Five Bells La ME1 16 B3
Flack Gdns ME3 9 G4
Flamingo Cl ME5 23 H4
Flaxmans Ct ME7 17 E1
Fleet Rd ME1 23 E1
Flint Grn ME5 29 F2
Florence St ME2 11 H5
Florin Dr ME1 15 H4
Foord St ME1 16 A3
Fordwich Dr ME3 11 G3
Fordwich Grn ME8 18 D5
Forest Dr ME5 28 D3
Forestdale Rd ME5 29 E5
Foresters Cl ME5 28 D3
Forge La, Bredhurst ME7 30 B3
Forge La, Gillingham ME7 17 H1
Forge La, High Halstow ME3 5 A2
Forge La, Higham ME3 10 C3
Forge La, Upchurch ME9 20 D4
Formby Rd ME2 6 C4
Fort Pitt Hill ME1 3 A2
Fort Pitt St ME4 3 A3
Fort St ME1 16 B4
Fostington Way ME5 28 C4
Foulds Cl ME8 25 G6
Foundry La ME7 18 A1
Fountain Rd ME2 11 E5
Four Elms Hill ME3 8 A6
Fourth Av ME7 18 A4
Fourwents Rd ME3 9 E3
Fowey Cl ME5 24 A5
Fowler Cl ME8 30 D2
Fox St ME7 17 F2
Foxburrow Cl ME8 25 H5
Foxglove Cres ME5 23 F6
Foxtail Cl ME4 13 F4
Francis Dr ME5 29 E3
Franklin Rd ME7 17 G3
Franks Ct ME8 18 C6
Freasia Cl ME7 18 A2
Frederick Rd ME7 17 F4
Freeman Gdns ME4 16 D6
Frensham Walk ME5 28 D3
Freshwater Rd ME5 23 H3
Friars Av ME5 28 D3
Friary Pl ME2 11 H6
Frindsbury Hill ME2 12 A4
Frindsbury Rd ME2 11 H6
Frinsted Cl ME8 19 E5
Friston Way ME1 23 E2
Frittenden Rd ME2 12 B4
Frobisher Gdns ME1 16 A6
Frost Cres ME5 23 H3
Fry Cl ME3 4 C5
Fulmar Rd ME2 14 D2
Furrells Rd ME1 3 D6

Gads Hill ME7 18 B1
Gainsborough Cl ME8 26 A4
Galahad Av ME2 15 E1
Galbri Dr ME2 15 G1
Galena Cl ME5 29 E4
Galleon Cl ME1 22 D3
Gardenia Cl ME2 11 H4
Gardiner St ME7 17 G2
Garfield Rd ME7 17 H1
Gas House Rd ME1 3 C4
Gatcombe Cl ME5 23 H6
Gate Rd ME4 13 G5
Gatekeeper Chase ME8 26 B2
Gayhurst Cl ME8 25 H4
Gean Cl ME5 29 E4
Geneva Av ME8 18 C5
Gentian Cl ME5 28 C1
George La ME1 3 B4
George Summers Cl ME2 12 C5
Georgian Way ME8 30 D1
Gerald Av ME4 16 D6
Gerrard Av ME1 23 E2
Gibraltar Av ME7 17 E1
Gibraltar Hill ME4 3 B3
Gifford Cl ME8 19 E4
Gilbert Cl ME7 25 E5
Gill Av ME2 12 B3
Gillingham Grn ME7 18 A1
Gillingham Rd ME7 17 G4
Gills Cotts ME1 16 B3
Gills Ct ME2 12 B6
Gills Ter ME8 20 B5
Ginsbury Cl ME2 16 C2
Gladstone Rd ME4 16 C5
Gladwyn Cl ME8 25 H6
Glamford Rd ME2 15 E2
Glamis Cl ME5 23 H5
Glanville Rd, Gillingham ME7 17 H3
Glanville Rd, Strood ME2 11 G6
Gleaming Wood Dr ME5 29 G5
Gleanings Mews ME1 3 A6
Glebe Rd ME7 18 A5
Glencoe Rd ME4 16 D5
Glenwood Cl, Hempstead ME7 25 E4
Glenwood Cl, Luton ME5 24 B2
Glistening Glade ME8 26 A4
Globe La ME4 3 B1
Glouscester Cl ME8 26 C2
Glovers Mill ME1 16 A4
Glynne Cl ME8 26 A5
Goad Av ME5 29 F1
Goddings Dr ME1 15 G5
Goddington Rd ME2 11 H5
Godfrey Cl ME2 11 F4
Goldcrest Dr ME4 13 F3
Golden Wood Cl ME5 29 G4
Goldsmith Rd ME8 26 A6
Goldstone Walk ME5 29 E4
Goldsworth Dr ME2 11 G4
Goodall Cl ME8 26 A5
Goodwin Rd ME3 7 F2
Goodwood Cl ME3 5 A2
Goose Cl ME5 23 H4
Gordon Rd, Brompton ME7 17 E1
Gordon Rd, Chatham ME4 17 E6
Gordon Rd, Gillingham ME7 17 H3
Gordon Rd, Hoo St Werburgh ME3 9 E4
Gordon Rd, Strood ME2 11 G6
Gordon Ter ME1 16 A3
Gore Green Rd ME3 7 A3
Gorse Av ME5 23 F6
Gorse Rd ME2 11 F5
Gorst St ME7 17 G3
Goudhurst Rd ME8 18 C5
Gould Rd ME5 29
Grafton Av ME1 23
Grain Ct ME8 30
Grain Rd, Grain ME3 4
Grain Rd, Lower Stoke ME3 5
Grain Rd, Wigmore ME8 30
Grainey Field ME9 27
Granary Cl ME8 26
Grandsire Gdns ME3 9
Grange Hill ME5 17
Grange Rd, Gillingham ME7 18
Grange Rd, Strood ME2 11
Grange Way ME1 16
Grant Cl ME8 25
Grant Rd ME3 12
Granville Rd ME7 17
Grasmere Gro ME2 12
Grassy Glade ME7 25
Gravel Walk ME1 16
Graveney Cl ME3 7
Gravesend Rd ME3 10
Grayne Av ME3 4
Great Lines ME7 17
Great South Av ME4 23
Grebe Cl ME3 5
Green Bank Cl ME7 25
Green Cl ME1 16
Green La, Cliffe ME3 6
Green La, Grain ME3 4
Green St ME7 17
Greenacre Cl ME5 23
Greenbank ME5 24
Greenfield Rd ME7 17
Greenfields Cl ME3 12
Greenfinches ME7 25
Greensands ME5 29
Greenvale Gdns ME8 18
Greenview Walk ME7 18
Greenway ME5 23
Greenwich Cl ME5 24
Gregory Cl ME8 26
Grenadier Cl ME8 20
Gresham Cl ME8 26
Grizedale Cl ME1 23
Grosvenor Av ME4 16
Grosvenor Rd ME8 25
Grove Rd, Gillingham ME7 18
Grove Rd, Luton ME4 17
Grove Rd, Strood ME2 11
Grove Rd, Upper Halling ME2 6
Guardian Ct ME8 25
Guildford Gdns ME2 14
Gun La ME2 11
Gundulph Rd ME4 3
Gundulph Sq ME1 3
Gunnis Cl ME8 25
Gypsy Way ME3 5

Hadleigh Ct ME7 30
Haig Av, Gillingham ME7 17
Haig Av, Luton ME4 17
Haig Av, Rochester ME1 23
Haig Villas ME3 8
Hale Rd ME3 7
Half Moon Way ME3 5
Halifax Cl ME5 24
Hall Rd ME5 29
Halling By-Pass 6
Hallsfield Rd ME5 28
Hallwood Cl ME8 25
Halstow La ME9 21
Ham La ME7 29
Ham River Hill ME3 7
Hamelin Rd ME7 24

milton Ct ME5 24 B1
milton Rd ME7 17 G1
mond Hill ME4 3 A2
mpshire Cl ME5 24 B3
mpton Cl ME5 23 H5
mwick Grn ME5 29 F3
ncock Cl ME2 11 H4
nover Dr ME8 30 D1
nway ME8 18 B6
rcourt Gdns ME8 26 A6
rdinge Cl ME8 25 H6
rds Town ME4 3 D3
rdy Cl ME5 24 A4
re St ME4 17 E5
rebell Cl ME5 23 F6
redale Cl ME1 23 E3
rlech Cl ME2 11 F4
rman Ct ME5 29 E2
rold Av ME7 17 H3
rold Rd ME2 14 C5
rp Farm Rd ME5 29 G5
rptree Dr ME5 23 F5
rrison Dr ME3 5 A1
rrow Rd ME7 25 E4
rtington St ME4 17 E5
rtlip Hill ME9 27 G3
rtpiece Cl ME8 19 G6
rty Av ME8 30 D1
rvel Av ME2 11 F6
rvesters Cl ME8 26 A4
rvey Rd ME8 26 A2
rwood Rd ME8 26 D1
tfield Rd ME2 11 G5
thaway Ct ME1 3 A6
tton Rd ME5 29 G2
ven Cl ME1 16 A6
ven St ME3 7 F4
ven Way ME4 13 F4
visham Cl ME1 16 A6
wbeck Rd ME8 31 E1
wkenbury Rise ME3 11 H3
wkhurst Rd ME8 18 C4
wkins Cl ME4 16 D2
wkwood Cl ME1 16 B3
wser Rd ME1 22 D1
wthorn Rd ME2 15 E2
wthorne Av ME8 18 D6
wthorns ME5 28 D3
yes Cl ME3 10 C2
yfields ME5 29 H3
yley Cl ME2 14 C5
ymen St ME4 16 C5
yward Av ME2 11 H5
zel Gro ME5 24 A2
zlemere Dr ME7 18 B2
adcorn Rd ME8 18 D4
ather Cl ME5 23 G6
athfield Cl ME5 24 A3
llyar Ct ME1 16 A4
mpstead Rd ME7 25 E5
mpstead Valley Dr ME7 25 F4
nley Cl, Rainham ME8 26 A2
nley Cl, Wayfield ME5 23 H4
nry St, Chatham ME4 17 F5
nry St, Rainham ME8 26 C1
pplewhite Mews ME5 28 D4
rbert Rd, Chatham ME4 17 E5
rbert Rd, Rainham ME8 26 A2
rberts Ct ME3 5 C4
rdsdown ME3 9 E4
reford Cl ME8 19 F6
ritage Dr ME7 24 D1
Heritage Rd ME5 23 H4
Herman Ter ME4 17 E5
Hermitage Rd ME3 10 C2
Herne Rd ME8 18 D6
Hero Walk ME1 22 D3
Heron Cl ME9 21 G4
Heron Way, Lower Stoke ME3 5 C5
Heron Way, Wayfield ME5 23 H5
Hertsfield Av ME3 11 G3
Herying Cl ME2 6 D6
Hever Croft ME2 15 F2
Hewitt Cl ME7 18 B2
Hickory Dell ME7 25 F5
Higgins La ME4 3 B1
High Bank ME1 16 B6
High Dewar Rd ME8 26 C2
High Elms ME8 19 F6
High St Chatham ME4 3 A2
High St Rochester ME1 3 C6
High St, Brompton ME7 17 E1
High St, Chatham ME4 3 B2
High St, Gillingham ME7 17 F2
High St, Grain ME3 4 C5
High St, Halling ME2 6 C5
High St, Lower Stoke ME3 5 C5
High St, Rainham ME8 26 B2
High St, Rochester ME1 3 B4
High St, Strood ME2 11 H6
High St, Upper Upnor ME2 12 D4
High Vw ME3 10 C1
Higham Rd, Cliffe ME3 6 A3
Higham Rd, Wainscott ME3 12 B2
Highfield Cl ME8 25 H3
Highfield Rd ME8 25 H3
Highgrove Rd ME5 23 H6
Highlands Cl ME2 14 D2
Highridge ME7 24 D1
Highview Dr ME5 23 E5
Highwoods Cl ME3 10 C1
Hilary Gdns ME1 15 F6
Hilda Rd ME4 16 D4
Hill Chase ME5 28 C2
Hill Ct ME3 8 B5
Hill Farm Cl ME3 5 A3
Hill Rd ME1 22 A5
Hill Rd, Rochester ME1 15 G6
Hill View Cotts ME3 5 A2
Hill View Way ME5 23 F5
Hillborough Gro ME5 29 E1
Hillcrest Dr ME2 14 C6
Hillcrest Rd ME4 16 C6
Hills Ter ME4 3 B3
Hillshaw Cres ME2 14 D3
Hillside ME1 15 G6
Hillside Av ME2 11 H5
Hillside Rd ME4 17 E4
Hilltop Rd ME2 12 A4
Hillyfield Cl ME2 11 G4
Hilton Rd ME3 7 F3
Hinton Cres ME7 25 E4
Hoath Cl ME8 25 F3
Hoath La ME8 25 F3
Hoath Way ME8 25 F1
Holborn La ME4 3 B1
Holcombe Rd, Chatham ME4 16 D6
Holcombe Rd, Rochester ME1 16 A5
Holder Cl ME5 24 A5
Holding St ME8 26 B2
Holland Rd ME5 23 E6
Hollingbourne Rd ME8 19 E5
Hollow La ME9 27 F5
Holly Cl, Gillingham ME7 18 A1
Holly Cl, Wayfield ME5 24 A2
Holly Rd, Strood ME2 15 E2
Holly Rd, Wainscott ME2 12 B3
Hollycroft ME2 14 C6
Hollytree Dr ME3 10 B2
Hollywood La ME3 11 H3
Holmes Cl ME3 5 B2
Holmoaks ME8 19 F6
Holmside ME7 17 H5
Holtwood Cl ME8 25 H5
Holywell La ME9 21 E5
Homefield Dr ME8 20 A6
Homewards Rd ME3 4 A2
Honey Cl ME7 25 E5
Honeybee Glade ME8 26 A5
Honeypot Cl ME2 11 H5
Honeysuckle Cl, Hempstead ME7 25 E6
Honeysuckle Cl, Walderslade ME5 28 C1
Hoo Common ME3 8 B5
Hoo Common Rd ME3 12 D1
Hoo Rd ME3 12 B2
Hook Cl ME5 23 F6
Hoopers Pl ME1 16 A3
Hoopers Rd ME1 16 A3
Hope St ME4 17 E5
Hopewell Dr ME5 24 B2
Hornbeam Av ME5 29 E2
Horrid Hill ME7 19 E2
Horse Wash La ME1 16 A1
Horseshoe Cl ME7 25 E5
Horsewash La ME1 3 B4
Horsham Hill ME8 20 C4
Horsham La ME8 20 B6
Horsley Rd ME1 15 H4
Horsted Av ME1 23 F1
Horsted Way ME1 23 E4
Horwood Cl ME1 22 C2
Hospital Hill ME7 25 F4
Hospital La ME1 16 C3
Hostier Cl ME2 6 D6
Hotel Rd ME8 18 B6
Hothfield Rd ME8 26 B1
Houghton Av ME7 30 C2
Howard Av ME1 16 B4
Howbury Walk ME8 25 H6
Howlsmere Cl ME2 6 D6
Huckleberry Cl ME5 29 F2
Hudson Cl ME8 25 G1
Hughes Dr ME2 12 A3
Hulkes La ME1 16 C3
Humber Cres ME2 15 F1
Hunstanton Cl ME8 31 F1
Hunters Way ME7 24 D1
Hunters Way West ME5 24 C1
Huntersfield Cl ME5 29 G3
Huntsmans Cl ME1 23 E1
Hurst Cl ME5 23 F4
Hurst Hill ME5 28 C3
Hurst Pl ME8 26 B2
Hurstwood ME5 23 F6
Hurstwood Rd ME7 30 C4
Hutsford Cl ME8 25 H5
Hyacinth Rd ME2 15 E1
Hybrid Cl ME1 23 E1
Hyperion Dr ME2 11 G4

Iden Rd ME2 12 A4
Idenwoodd Cl ME8 25 H5
Illustrious Cl ME5 23 H5
Imperial Rd ME7 17 F5
Impton La ME5 28 D5

INDUSTRIAL & RETAIL:
Airport Industrial Est ME1 22 D4
Altbarn Ind Centre ME5 29 G4
Arden Business Pk ME2 12 B6
Ballard Business Pk ME2 15 F3
Ballard Industrial Centre ME5 29 G4
Beechings Way Industrial Centre ME8 18 C3
Bridgewood Business Pk ME1 22 C3
Castle Vw Business Centre ME1 3 C4
Central Business Pk ME2 16 C1
Cuxton Industrial Est ME2 14 C6
Fine Line Industrial Est ME2 12 B6
Gillingham Business Pk ME8 25 E2
Horsted Retail Pk ME5 23 E5
Lakeside Park ME2 16 C1
Loaland Business Centre ME2 12 B5
Lords Wood Industrial Est ME5 29 G4
Medway Enterprise Centre ME2 12 B5
Meridian Park ME2 16 C1
Neptune Business Est ME2 12 C6
Newington Industrial Est ME9 27 H4
Northpoint Business Est ME2 12 B5
Oaks Business Village ME5 29 F4
Pentagon Shopping Centre ME4 3 B1
Phoenix Industrial Est ME2 12 A6
Riverside Est ME2 16 C2
Riverside One ME2 16 C1
Riverside Three ME2 16 C2
Riverside Two ME2 16 C2
Roman Way Industrial Est ME2 15 F3
Sextant Park ME2 16 C1
Spectrum Business Est ME2 12 B6
Temple Industrial Est ME2 15 H1
The Enterprise Centre ME5 29 G4
Victory Business Pk ME2 12 B6
Westfield Business Centre ME2 12 A6

Ingle Rd ME4 16 D6
Ingram Rd ME7 17 H2
Institute Rd ME4 17 E4
Iona Cl ME5 29 G4
Iris Cl ME5 29 E5
Ironside Cl ME5 23 H2
Irvine Rd ME3 10 C3
Island Way East ME4 13 F4
Island Way West ME4 13 E3
Islingham Farm Rd ME3 12 B2
Iversgate Cl ME8 19 G6
Ivy Pl ME1 15 G6
Ivy St ME8 26 B2

Jacklin Cl ME5 28 D2
Jackson Av ME1 23 F2
Jackson Cl ME8 25 H1
Jade Hill ME2 6 C4
James Rd ME2 14 C6
James St, Chatham ME4 3 C3
James St, Gillingham ME7 17 G2
James St, Rochester ME1 16 A4
Janton Cl ME3 7 F2
Japonica Cl ME5 29 G3
Jarrett Av ME2 12 A3
Jasmine Cl ME5 23 G6
Jasper Av ME1 16 A5
Jefferson Dr ME8 25 H2
Jeffery St ME7 17 G2
Jenkins Dale ME4 16 D5
Jenner Rd ME1 16 A4
Jennifer Ct ME3 9 G4
Jersey Rd ME2 11 G6
Jeyes Rd ME7 17 G4
Jezreels Rd ME7 17 G5
Jiniwin Rd ME1 23 E3
John St ME1 16 A3
Johnson Av ME7 13 F6
Joiners Ct ME4 17 E6
Jubilee Ter ME7 17 G2
Judkins Cl ME5 24 A4
Junction Rd ME7 17 H4
Juniper Cl ME5 23 G6
Jutland Cl ME3 4 B3

Katherine Ct ME5 29 E2
Keefe Cl ME5 28 B3
Keeley Mews ME7 18 A5
Kellaway Rd ME5 29 E2
Kelly Dr ME7 13 G6
Kemp Cl ME5 28 B1
Kempton Cl ME5 29 G2
Kemsley Street Rd ME7 30 D3
Kendal Way ME8 25 H2
Kenilworth Dr ME8 25 H4
Kenilworth Gdns ME8 25 H4
Kennard Cl ME1 15 F6
Kennington Cl ME8 18 D4
Kent Cl ME1 22 D2
Kent Rd ME2 6 C4
Kent Ter ME8 20 B6
Kenwood Av ME5 23 H6
Kenyon Walk ME8 30 D1
Kesteven Cl ME2 6 D5
Keston Ct ME8 18 B6
Kestrel Rd ME5 29 G3
Keyes Av ME4 16 D6
Khartoum Rd ME4,7 16 D2
Khyber Rd ME4 13 E6
Killick Rd ME3 9 F4
Kimberley Rd ME7 17 G4
King Arthurs Dr ME2 11 G4
King Edward Rd, Chatham ME4 16 C5
King Edward Rd, Gillingham ME7 18 A2
King Edward Rd, Rochester ME1 3 B6
King George Rd ME5 23 F6
King St, Chatham ME4 3 C2
King St, Gillingham ME7 17 G2
King St, Rochester ME1 16 A3
King William Rd ME7 13 G6
Kingfisher Dr ME5 24 A3
Kings Av ME1 16 A4
Kings Bastion ME7 17 E2
Kings Orchard ME1 3 B5
Kings Rd ME5 24 B1
Kingsdale Ct ME5 24 B1
Kingsdown Cl ME7 25 F6
Kingshill Dr ME3 9 F3
Kingsnorth Cl ME3 9 G4
Kingsnorth Rd ME8 18 D4
Kingston Cres ME5 24 A6
Kingsway ME5 24 C1
Kingswear Gdns ME2 12 A6

Kingswood Av ME4 16 C6
Kingswood Rd, Gillingham ME7 17 G2
Kingswood Rd, Kit's Coty ME20 28 B5
Kinross Cl ME5 24 A3
Kirby Rd ME3 8 B4
Kirkdale Cl ME5 29 H3
Kit Hill Av ME5 28 C1
Kitchener Av ME4 23 G1
Kitchener Cotts ME3 5 C5
Kitchener Rd, Chattenden ME3 8 B5
Kitchener Rd, Strood ME2 11 G5
Knavesacre Ct ME8 25 H6
Knight Av ME7 17 H1
Knight Rd ME2 15 G1
Knights Cl ME3 9 F4
Knights Rd ME3 9 E4
Knole Rd ME5 29 G2

Laburnum Rd ME2 15 E3
Ladyclose Av ME3 7 E2
Ladyfields ME5 29 H3
Ladywood Rd ME2 14 B5
Lake Dr ME3 7 A3
Laker Rd ME1 22 D4
Lakeside Ct ME2 16 C1
Lakewood Dr ME8 25 G5
Lambarde Cl ME2 6 C6
Lamberhurst Grn ME8 18 C5
Lambes Ct ME8 25 H5
Lambeth Cl ME5 24 A6
Lambourn Way ME5 29 G2
Lambourne Pl ME8 19 H6
Lambsfrith Gro ME7 30 C1
Lamplighters Cl ME7 25 E5
Lancaster Ct ME8 25 G3
Lancelot Av ME2 11 E6
Lancelot Cl ME2 15 E1
Landor Ct ME7 30 C2
Landrail Rd ME9 21 F5
Landway ME3 7 A4
Langdale Cl ME8 19 E6
Langdon Rd ME1 16 A4
Lankester Parker Rd ME1 22 D5
Lansdowne Rd ME4 16 C6
Laping Dr ME9 21 G5
Lapwing Rd ME3 4 C6
Larch Wood Cl ME5 29 G4
Larchcroft ME5 23 H6
Larkfield Av ME7 17 H4
Larkin Cl ME2 11 H3
Larkspur Rd ME5 28 C1
Laser Quay ME2 16 B1
Latimer Pl ME7 17 G1
Laura Pl ME1 15 G6
Laurel Rd ME7 13 G6
Laurel Walk ME8 26 A4
Laurie Gray Av ME5 28 B4
Lavenda Cl ME7 25 E6
Lavender Cl ME5 23 F6
Lawn Cl ME4 17 F6
Lawrence St ME7 17 G3
Layfield Rd ME7 18 A1
Leafy Glade ME8 25 G5
Leaman Cl ME3 5 B2
Leander Rd ME1 22 D3
Leander Walk ME1 22 D3
Lee Green Rd ME3 7 E3
Leeds Sq ME8 18 C5
Leet Cl ME7 18 A1
Leeward Rd ME1 22 D1
Leigh Rd ME3 12 A2
Leitch Row ME7 17 E1
Lenham Way ME8 18 C5
Lennox Row ME7 17 E1
Leonard Rd ME4 17 F5
Leopold Rd ME4 16 D5
Leslie Rd ME7 13 H6
Lester Rd ME4 17 E5
Letchworth Av ME4 23 F1
Levett Cl ME3 4 C5
Lewis Av ME8 18 C5
Leybourne Cl ME5 29 E3
Leybourne Rd ME2 11 F6
Leyton Av ME7 24 D1
Lichfield Cl ME8 19 E5
Lidsing Rd ME7 30 A2
Lilac Cres ME2 15 E2
Lilac Rd ME2 15 E2
Lillechurch Rd ME3 7 C2
Lime Ct ME8 30 D2
Limetree Cl ME5 24 A3
Lincoln Cl ME2 14 D2
Lincoln Rd ME7 17 G1
Linden Rd ME7 17 H3
Lineacre Cl ME8 25 H5
Lines Ter ME4 3 D2
Lingley Dr ME2 12 A3
Linton Dann Cl ME3 9 E3
Lintorn Simmonds Rd ME3 8 B4
Linwood Av ME2 11 E5
Listmas Rd ME4 17 E5
Little John Av ME5 28 D3
Little Oakham Ct ME3 5 C5
Littlebourne Av ME8 18 C4
Littlefield Rd ME8 20 A6
Livingstone Circus ME7 17 H3
Livingstone Rd ME7 17 H3
Lobelia Cl ME7 18 A2
Locarno Av ME8 18 C5
Lochat Rd ME3 8 A3
Lock St ME7 17 F2
Lockington Gro ME1 16 A3
Lodge Hill La ME3 8 B2
London Rd, Hartlip ME9 27 F3
London Rd, Rainham ME8 25 F1
London Rd, Strood ME2 11 G6
Long Catlis Rd ME8 25 H6
Longfellow Rd ME7 17 F5
Longfield Av ME3 5 A2
Longford Cl ME8 26 C2
Longhill Av ME5 17 F4
Longhurst Dr ME5 28 D3
Longley Rd, Rainham ME8 26 B2
Longley Rd, Rochester ME1 16 A4
Longwood ME5 29 F4
Lonsdale Dr ME8 26 A5
Lords Wood Cl ME5 29 F3
Lords Wood La ME5 24 A6
Louisville Av ME7 17 H4
Love La ME1 3 A6
Lovelace Cl ME8 25 H6
Low Meadow ME2 6 C5
Lower Bloors La ME8 19 F5
Lower East Rd ME4 13 F5
Lower Featherby Rd ME7 18 C3
Lower Hartlip Rd ME9 27 F6
Lower Rainham Rd ME7,8 18 C2
Lower Robin Hood La ME5 28 C3
Lower Rochester Rd ME3 7 A3
Lower Twydall La ME8 18 D4
Lower Woodlands Rd ME7 18 B2
Lubbock Walk ME8 26 A6
Lullingstone Cl ME7 30 C2
Lumsden Ter ME4 3 A3
Luton High St ME5 17 G6
Luton Rd ME4 17 E4
Lyall Way ME8 26 A6
Lychfield Dr ME2 11 G5
Lydd Rd ME5 24 A5
Lyle Cl ME2 11 H5
Lyminge Cl ME8 18 D5
Lyndhurst Av ME8 25 G3
Lynette Av ME2 11 G4
Lynors Av ME2 11 G4
Lynsted Rd ME8 18 C4
Lynton Dr ME5 29 F2

Macdonald Rd ME7 17 H1
Mackintosh Cl ME3 5 B2
Macklands Way ME8 19 H6
Madden Av ME5 23 F6
Mafeking Rd ME5 28 D2
Magdalen Cl ME7 30 B1
Magnolia Av ME8 25 F6
Magpie Hall Rd ME4 17 E4
Magpie La ME9,14 31 F4
Magwitch Cl ME1 15 H4
Maida Rd ME4 17 F6
Maidstone Rd, Chatham ME4 3 B3
Maidstone Rd, Rochester ME1 16 A5
Maidstone Rd, Walderslade ME5 23 E6
Maidstone Rd, Wigmore ME8 30 D2
Main Gate Rd ME4 16 D1
Main Rd ME3 8 C5
Mallard Way ME3 5 C5
Mallingdene Cl ME3 7 F1
Mallow Way ME5 23 F6
Malmaynes Hall Rd ME3 5 A6
Malt Mews ME1 3 B6
Malta Av ME5 23 G3
Malus Cl ME5 29 E4
Malvern Rd ME7 17 H5
Manchester Cl ME5 24 A4
Manor Gdns ME5 28 D1
Manor La ME1 15 F5
Manor Rd ME4 3 A2
Manor St ME7 17 E1
Mansell Dr ME1 15 G5
Mansion Row ME7 17 E2
Maple Av ME7 18 A2
Maple Rd ME2 15 F1
Maplins Cl ME8 26 B2
Marathon Paddock ME7 17 H3
Marc Brunel Way ME4 13 E6
Marconi Way ME1 23 E4
Mardale Cl ME8 26 C2
Marden Rd ME2 12 A4
Margate Cl ME7 18 A1
Margetts Pl ME2 8 C6
Marine Vw ME4 13 F4
Marion Cl ME5 29 E2
Maritime Cl ME2 12 B5
Maritime Way ME4 13 E5
Market Pl ME1 3 C4
Marlborough Rd ME7 17 F3
Marley Rd ME3 9 F3
Marley Way ME1 16 A6
Marlow Copse ME5 28 D3
Marquis Dr ME7 30 C2
Marsh Cres ME3 5 A1
Marsh La ME3 6 C1
Marsh Rd ME2 6 C5
Marsh St ME2 11 H6
Marshall Rd ME8 25 G2
Marsham Way ME2 6 D5
Marshland Vw ME3 5 C4
Marstan Cl, Upchurch ME9 20 D5
Marston Cl, Walderslade ME5 28 C2
Marston Walk ME5 28 C2
Martin Ct ME7 30 C2
Martin Rd ME2 11 H6
Martins Cl ME3 7 A3
Maryland Ct ME8 26 A6
Masefield Dr ME3 7 F2
Matilda Cl ME8 25 F2
Matts Hill Rd ME9 31 E3
Maunders Cl ME5 24 A2
Maximilian Dr ME2 6 D5
Maxwell Rd ME7 17 E2
May Rd, Gillingham ME7 17 F3
May Rd, Rochester ME1 16 A5
May St ME2 14 C6
Mayfair Cl ME2 12 A5
Mayfield Cl, Eastcourt ME8 19 F6
Mayfield Cl, Lords Wood ME5 29 E4
Mayford Rd ME5 29 H3
Maynard Pl ME5 17 H6
Mayweed Av ME5 23 F6
McKenzie Rd ME5 29 E2
Mead Grn ME5 29 F2
Mead Wall ME3 6 A1
Meadow Bank Rd ME4 17 E4
Meadow Cl, Upper Halling ME2 6 A6
Meadow Cl, Walderslade ME5 23 G5
Meadow Cres ME2 6 A6
Meadowdown Cl ME7 25 F6
Meadowsweet View ME4 13 F4
Meadside Walk ME5 23 G5
Medlar Gro ME7 25 F6
Medway Av ME3 5 B1
Medway Gdns ME4 12 D6
Medway Rd, Gillingham ME7 13 F6
Medway Rd, Rainham ME8 26 B1
Medway St ME4 3 B1
Medway Tunnel ME2 12 D5
Meeting House La ME4 3 C2
Megby Cl ME8 25 H4
Melbourne Rd ME4 17 E5
Melody Cl ME8 30 D1
Melville Ct ME4 16 D2
Mercury Cl ME1 15 G5
Meresborough La ME8 26 C5
Meresborough Rd ME8 26 C4
Mereworth Cl ME8 18 C4
Merivale Gro ME5 23 H6
Mermaid Cl ME5 23 H4
Merrals Wood Rd ME2 14 D3
Merryboys Rd ME3 7 E1
Merryfields ME2 11 G4
Merton Cl ME5 24 B6
Micawber Cl ME5 28 D4
Middle St ME7 17 E1
Middlefields ME8 26 C2
Middleton Cl ME8 26 A6
Mierscourt Cl ME8 26 C2
Mierscourt Rd ME8 26 B3
Milburn Rd ME7 17 G1
Miles Pl ME1 16 B4
Military Rd ME4 3 B2
Mill Cl ME2 11 H5
Mill Hill ME9 27 H2
Mill La, Blue Bell Hill ME5 28 B4
Mill La, Hartlip ME9 27 G4
Mill La, Wayfield ME5 24 B1
Mill Rd, Frindsbury ME2 11 H5
Mill Rd, Gillingham ME7 17 F2
Millcroft Rd ME3 6 B2
Miller Way ME2 12 A3
Millfields ME5 29 H3
Millfordhope Rd ME2 10 C6
Millpond Cl ME2 11 H5
Mills Ter ME4 17 E5
Milner Rd ME7 17
Milsted Rd ME8 18
Milton Av ME3 7
Milton Rd ME7 17
Mincers Cl ME5 29
Minerva Rd ME2 11
Minor Canon Row ME1 3
Minster Rd ME8 18
Miskin Rd ME3 9
Mitchell Av ME4 16
Mitre Rd ME1 15
Monarch Cl ME5 23
Monkwood Cl ME1 22
Monmouth Cl ME8 19
Montford Rd ME5 28
Montfort Rd ME2 11
Montgomery Av ME5 23
Montgomery Rd ME7 17
Montrose Av ME5 17
Moonstone Dr ME5 29
Moor Park Cl ME8 26
Moor St ME8 26
Moore St ME2 11
Mooring Rd ME1 23
Morden St ME1 16
Morement Rd ME3 9
Morgan Cl ME8 26
Morgan Rd ME2 11
Morland Dr ME2 11
Morning Cross Cotts ME3 6
Mortimers Av ME3 7
Mossbank ME5 29
Mossy Glade ME8 26
Motney Hill Rd ME8 19
Mouat Ct ME5 29
Mount La ME9 27
Mount Pleasant ME5 17
Mount Rd, Borstal ME1 15
Mount Rd, Chatham ME4 16
Mountbatten Av, Higham ME3 10
Mountbatten Av, Wayfield ME5 23
Moyle Cl ME8 26
Mozart Ct ME4 16
Mulberry Cl ME7 25
Munns La ME9 27
Murray Rd ME2 12
Myrtle Cres ME5 23

Nags Head La ME1 16
Napier Rd ME7 17
Napwood Cl ME8 25
Nares Rd ME8 31
Nash Cl ME5 29
Nashenden Farm La ME1 22
Nashenden La ME1 15
Natal Rd ME4 16
Naylors Cotts ME7 30
Neale St ME4 16
Nelson Ct ME5 24
Nelson Rd ME7 17
Nelson Ter ME5 24
Neptune Cl ME2 16
Neptune Way ME2 16
Neville Rd ME4 16
New Covenant Pl ME1 16
New Cut ME4 3
New Rd, Chatham ME4 3
New Rd, Cliffe ME3 6
New Rd, Rochester ME1 16
New Road Av ME4 3
New St ME4 16
New Stairs ME4 16
Newark Ct*, North St ME2 11
Newark Yard ME2 11

wbury Cl ME3 7 E1
wenden Rd ME2 12 A4
witt Rd ME3 9 F4
wnham Cl ME8 19 E5
wnham St ME4 17 E5
wton Cl ME5 29 G3
klaus Dr ME5 28 D2
kleby Cl ME1 16 A6
htingale Cl ME8 26 A4
e Rd ME7 17 G4
e Acres Rd ME2 14 B5
en Cl ME3 12 A2
rah La ME3 10 B1
re Cl ME7 24 C1
rfolk Cl, Eastcourt ME8 19 E6
rfolk Cl, Lords Wood ME5 29 F2
rman Cl, Strood ME2 15 F3
rman Cl, Wigmore ME8 25 F6
rreys Rd ME8 26 A3
rth Bank Cl ME2 15 F2
rth Dane Rd ME5 24 B4
rth Rd, Brompton ME7 17 E1
rth Rd, Cliffe ME3 6 B1
rth Side Three Rd ME4 13 F5
rth St ME2 11 H6
rthbourne Rd ME8 18 C4
rthcote Rd ME2 15 G1
rthgate ME1 3 B5
rthumberland Av ME8 26 B1
rthwood Av ME3 5 A1
rton Gro ME5 28 C1
rwich Cl ME2 14 D2
rwood Cl ME3 6 B3
ttingham Walk ME2 14 D2
rsery Gdns ME3 9 G5
rsery Rd ME8 25 H2
tfield Cl ME5 24 A2

k Av ME7 18 A2
k Dr ME3 10 C2
k La ME9 20 C6
k Rd ME2 15 E2
khurst Cl ME5 28 D1
kland Cl ME5 28 D1
kleigh Cl ME5 28 C2
ks Dene ME5 28 D4
kum Ct ME4 17 F6
stview ME8 26 C2
tavia Ct ME5 29 E1
icers Rd ME4 13 E6
d Barn Cl ME7 25 E5
d Castle Walk ME8 31 F1
d Chatham Rd ME20 28 B6
d George Ct ME3 8 B5
d Guard Ho ME3 4 C6
d House Rd ME9 27 G6
d Pattens La ME1 16 B5
d Rd ME4 3 B3
d School Ct ME3 8 B5
d Watling St ME2 10 B6
dcastle Walk ME8 26 A6
dfield Cl ME8 25 H2
ver Cl ME4 17 F6
ver Twist Cl ME1 15 H4
vine Cl ME5 29 E4
ffes Cl ME5 28 D3
slow Rd ME1 16 B5
al Grn ME5 29 F3
ange Ter ME1 16 B3
bit Cl ME5 29 E5
chard Av ME2 11 F5
chard St ME8 26 A3
chard Villas ME4 3 C3
chid Cl ME2 14 C1

Ordnance St ME4 3 A3
Ordnance Ter ME4 3 A3
Orion Rd ME1 22 D3
Ormsby Grn ME8 31 F1
Osborne Rd ME7 17 G3
Osprey Av ME5 17 H6
Otterham Quay La ME8 26 D2
Otway St, Chatham ME4 17 E5
Otway St, Gillingham ME7 17 G2
Otway Ter ME4 17 E5
Owens Way ME7 18 B1
Oxford Rd ME7 17 H4

Packer Pl ME5 23 H3
Paget Row ME7 17 F3
Paget St ME7 17 F3
Pagitt St ME4 16 C6
Palace Ct ME5 17 H5
Palmers Ter ME3 5 C4
Palmerston Rd ME4 16 D6
Pankhurst Rd ME3 9 E3
Pannell Rd ME3 4 C5
Panton Cl ME5 29 F1
Papion Gro ME5 28 C3
Parham Rd ME4 16 D6
Park Av ME7 17 H5
Park Cres ME4 23 G2
Parker Cl ME8 26 A5
Parkfield Rd ME8 19 G6
Parkfields ME2 10 C6
Parkside ME3 7 E2
Parkwood Grn ME8 25 H5
Parr Av ME7 17 H1
Parsonage La ME2 12 A5
Partridge Dr ME4 13 E4
Partridge Rise ME4 13 F3
Pasley Rd ME7 17 E1
Pasley Rd East ME7 13 E6
Pasley Rd North ME7 13 E6
Pasley Rd West ME7 13 E6
Patrixbourne Av ME8 18 D6
Pattens Gdns ME1 16 B6
Pattens La ME4 16 B6
Pattens Pl ME1 16 B6
Patterns La ME1 23 E1
Payne Ct ME8 31 E1
Peal Cl ME3 9 G4
Pear Tree La ME7 24 C2
Pearman Cl ME8 26 C1
Peartree La ME3 10 A4
Peckham Cl ME2 12 A5
Peggoty Cl ME3 10 C2
Pelican Cl ME2 14 C1
Pemberton Sq ME2 12 A5
Pembroke Gdns ME8 26 A6
Pembroke Rd ME4 13 E6
Pembury Way ME8 19 F6
Penfold Cl ME5 23 H3
Penguin Cl ME2 14 D1
Pennant Rd ME1 22 D3
Penshurst Cl ME8 19 F6
Pepys Way ME2 11 G6
Perry St ME4 16 C5
Peterborough Gdns ME2 14 D2
Petham Green ME8 18 D5
Peverel Grn ME8 31 E1
Pheasant Rd ME4 17 F6
Phillips Ct ME8 18 D6
Phoenix Rd ME5 29 F3
Pickles Way ME3 6 A1
Pickwick Cres ME1 16 A5
Pier Approach Rd ME7 13 G6
Pier Pl ME2 12 D3
Pier Rd ME7 13 H6
Pikefields ME8 18 D5
Pilgrims Rd ME2 6 A4
Pilgrims Way ME2 14 C5

Pilot Rd ME1 22 D2
Pimpernel Way ME5 23 F6
Pine Gro ME7 25 E5
Pine Rd ME2 15 F2
Pinewood Dr ME5 29 H4
Pintail Cl ME3 4 C5
Pippin Croft ME7 25 F4
Pirbright Cl ME5 29 H3
Place La ME9 27 E5
Plantation Rd ME7 18 B2
Pleasant Row ME7 16 D1
Plomley Cl ME8 31 E1
Ploughman Way ME5 29 E4
Ploughmans Way ME8 26 A4
Plover Cl ME5 29 G3
Pluckley Cl ME8 18 D4
Plumtree Gro ME7 25 E6
Poachers Cl ME5 24 A5
Polhill Dr ME5 28 D3
Pond Hill ME3 6 B1
Poot La ME9 20 D3
Poplar Cl ME2 15 F3
Poplar Rd ME2 15 E3
Poplicans Rd ME2 14 B5
Poppy Cl ME7 18 A2
Port Cl ME5 29 F2
Port Rise ME4 16 D5
Port Victoria Rd ME3 4 D6
Portland Rd ME7 17 H2
Portland St ME4 17 E5
Portree Mews ME7 18 A5
Portsmouth Cl ME2 14 D2
Portway Rd ME3 7 F2
Post Barn Rd ME4 16 D6
Pottery Rd ME3 9 F4
Povey Av ME2 12 A3
Powlett Rd ME2 12 A5
Preston Av ME7 24 D1
Preston Way ME8 18 D6
Pretoria Rd, Chatham ME4 16 D6
Pretoria Rd, Gillingham ME7 17 G4
Priestfield Rd ME7 17 H3
Priestfields ME1 15 H5
Primrose Av ME8 25 G6
Primrose Cl ME4 23 F3
Primrose Rd ME2 6 A5
Prince Arthur Rd ME7 17 E1
Prince Charles Av ME5 23 H6
Princes Av ME5 28 D1
Princes St ME1 16 A4
Princess Mary Av ME7 13 F6
Prinys Dr ME8 30 D1
Priory Ct ME8 18 B6
Priory Rd, Strood ME2 15 G1
Priory Rd, Twdall ME8 18 B5
Prospect Av ME2 11 H5
Prospect Pl ME1 15 G6
Prospect Row, Brompton ME7 17 E2
Prospect Row, Chatham ME4 16 D4
Providence La ME1 3 C5
Pudding Rd ME8 26 C2
Puffin Rd ME3 4 C5
Pump La ME8 19 E6
Purbeck Rd ME4 16 C6
Purser Way ME7 13 G6
Pyrus Cl ME5 29 E4

Queen St, Chatham ME4 3 C2
Queen St, Rochester ME1 16 A4
Queendown Av ME8 25 H5
Queens Rd, Gillingham ME7 17 G3
Queens Rd, Luton ME5 17 G6
Queensway ME3 4 C2
Queenswood Rd ME20 28 B6

Quickrells Av ME3 6 B1
Quickthorn Cres ME5 23 F5
Quinion Cl ME5 28 D4
Quinnell St ME8 26 B1
Quixote Cres ME2 11 H4

Radleigh Gdns ME1 23 F1
Railway St, Chatham ME4 3 B3
Railway St, Gillingham ME7 17 G2
Rainham Rd ME5 17 G5
Raleigh Cl ME5 23 H4
Ramillies Cl ME5 23 H5
Randall Rd ME4 23 F1
Randolph Cotts ME2 11 H4
Randolph Rd ME7 17 G3
Ranscombe Cl ME2 15 E3
Ratcliffe Highway, Chattenden ME3 8 C4
Ratcliffe Highway, Hallows ME3 4 A3
Ratcliffe Highway, High Halstow ME3 5 D3
Ravenswood Av ME2 11 H5
Readscroft Rd ME8 25 H6
Rectory Grange ME1 15 H6
Redbridge Cl ME5 24 A6
Rede Court Rd ME2 11 E6
Redfern Av ME7 18 A3
Redland Shaw ME1 23 F1
Redshank Rd ME4 13 E4
Redvers Rd ME4 16 D6
Redwing Rd ME5 24 A4
Redwood Cl ME5 29 E3
Reed St ME3 6 B1
Reedham Cres ME3 7 F2
Reform Rd ME4 17 F5
Regency Cl ME8 30 D2
Regent Rd ME7 17 F3
Reginald Av ME2 14 C5
Renown Rd ME5 29 F3
Repton Way ME5 28 D1
Resolution Cl ME5 23 H5
Revenge Rd ME5 29 F4
Reynolds Fields ME3 7 A3
Rhode St ME4 3 C3
Richard St, Chatham ME4 3 C2
Richard St, Rochester ME1 16 A4
Richborough Dr ME2 11 G4
Richmond Cl, Lords Wood ME5 24 A6
Richmond Cl, Wainscott ME2 12 D4
Richmond Rd ME7 17 G1
Ridley Rd ME1 15 H3
Ringwood Cl ME8 26 A3
Ripon Cl ME8 19 E5
River Dr ME2 11 F6
River Vw ME8 19 E5
Roach St ME2 15 G1
Roan Ct ME2 11 F6
Roberts Rd ME8 26 A2
Robin Hood La ME5 28 D3
Robson Dr ME3 9 F4
Rochester Av ME1 16 A4
Rochester Bri ME1 3 B4
Rochester Cl ME2 12 B6
Rochester Cres ME3 9 F3
Rochester Rd ME1 22 D5
Rochester St ME4 3 B3
Rock Av ME7 17 G4
Rodkin Wood ME5 28 D4
Roebuck Rd ME1 16 A3
Roffen Rd ME1 16 A5
Rolvenden Av ME8 19 E5
Rolvenden Rd ME2 12 A3
Roman Cl ME5 28 B4

Roman Way ME2 15 F3
Romany Rd ME8 18 C6
Rome Ter ME4 3 B2
Romney Rd ME5 24 A5
Romsey Cl ME2 11 E5
Rookery Cres ME3 6 B1
Roosevelt Av ME5 23 G3
Rope Walk ME4 3 C1
Ropemakers Ct ME4 23 H1
Roper Cl ME8 31 E2
Ropers Green La ME3 5 D3
Ropers La ME3 9 G1
Rose St ME1 16 B4
Rosebery Rd, Chatham ME4 16 C6
Rosebery Rd, Gillingham ME7 17 G1
Rosemary Cl ME5 23 F6
Rosemount Ct ME2 11 G5
Ross St ME1 16 A3
Rother Vale ME5 29 F1
Roundwood Cl ME5 29 E4
Rover Rd ME5 29 F3
Rowan Lea ME5 24 A2
Rowan Walk ME4 16 C4
Rowbrocke Cl ME8 31 E2
Rowland Av ME7 24 D1
Rowland Cl ME7 24 C1
Royal Eagle Cl ME2 12 C6
Royal Sovereign Av ME4 13 F6
Roystons Cl ME8 19 G6
Ruckinge Way ME8 18 D5
Rudge Cl ME5 29 H3
Rugby Cl ME5 28 D1
Ruggles Cl ME3 5 B2
Rush Cl ME5 29 E2
Rushdean Rd ME2 14 D2
Russell Av ME8 26 C2
Russell Ct ME4 17 E5
Russell Rd ME20 28 A6
Russett Cl ME2 11 E5
Rutland Pl ME8 30 D1
Rycaut Cl ME8 31 E1
Ryde Cl ME5 24 A3
Rye St ME3 6 D1
Ryegrass Cl ME5 24 B4

Sabre Ct ME8 25 E1
Sadlers Cl ME5 28 B2
Saffron Way ME5 23 G6
Sage Rd ME1 15 G4
Sailmakers Ct ME4 17 E6
St Albans Cl ME7 17 H1
St Albans Rd ME2 14 D2
St Albans Walk ME4 16 C5
St Andrews Rd ME7 13 G6
St Andrews Walk ME3 4 C3
St Barnabas Cl ME7 17 H4
St David Rd ME3 4 C3
St Edmunds Way ME8 26 C1
St Georges Rd ME7 17 G1
St Georges Walk ME3 4 C3
St Helens Rd ME3 6 B2
St James Cl ME3 4 C5
St James Rd ME3 4 C5
St Johns Cl ME3 10 C2
St Johns Rd, Gillingham ME7 17 F5
St Johns Rd, Higham ME3 10 C1
St Johns Rd, Hoo St Werburgh ME3 9 F3
St Johns Way ME1 15 G6
St Leonards Av ME4 16 D6
St Lukes Way ME3 4 C3
St Margarets Bank ME1 3 C6
St Margarets Ct ME3 5 A2
St Margarets Dr ME8 25 G5
St Margarets Mews ME1 3 B5

St Margarets St ME1 3 B6
St Marys Gdns ME4 13 F6
St Marys Rd, Findsbury ME2 11 H6
St Marys Rd, Gillingham ME7 17 G1
St Matthews Dr ME1 15 G6
St Matthews Way ME3 4 C3
St Michaels Cl ME4 16 C4
St Michaels Ct ME2 11 H6
St Nicholas Gdns ME2 11 F6
St Pauls Cl ME2 14 D2
St Peter St ME1 16 B4
St Stephens Mews ME1 23 F2
St Werburgh Cres ME3 9 E4
St Williams Way ME1 16 B5
Salisbury Av ME8 25 H2
Salisbury Rd, Chatham ME4 17 E4
Salisbury Rd, Kit's Coty ME20 28 A5
Sally Port Gardens ME7 17 E2
Salt La ME3 6 A3
Samara Cl ME5 29 E4
Sanctuary Rd ME8 18 B5
Sandgate Ct ME8 26 B6
Sandhill La ME3 7 B3
Sandhurst Cl ME8 18 D5
Sandling Way ME4 13 F4
Sandown Dr ME8 25 H4
Sandpiper Rd ME5 29 G3
Sandringham Rd ME8 31 F1
Sandstone Rise ME5 29 F5
Sandy Dell ME7 30 C2
Sandycroft Rd ME2 11 F5
Sappers Walk ME7 17 G2
Saracen Cl ME8 25 F1
Saracen Fields ME5 29 F5
Sarsen Heights ME5 28 D4
Saunders St, Chatham ME4 3 B3
Saunders St, Gillingham ME7 17 F1
Savage Rd ME5 29 F2
Sawyers Ct ME4 17 E6
Saxon Cl ME2 11 G4
Saxon Pl ME2 15 F3
Saxton St ME7 17 F3
Scarlett Cl ME5 24 A5
Scholars Rise ME2 14 D1
Scholey Cl ME2 6 D6
School Av ME7 17 H3
School La, Higham ME3 10 C2
School La, Lower Halstow ME9 21 G5
Scimitar Cl ME8 25 E2
Scotby Av ME5 23 H6
Scott Av ME8 26 C2
Scotteswood Av ME4 16 D6
Scotts Terr ME4 16 C5
Scragged Oak Rd ME14 31 E6
Seaford Ct*, Esplanade ME1 15 H3
Seagull Rd ME2 14 D1
Sealand Ct*, Esplanade ME1 15 H3
Seamew Ct*, Bligh Way ME2 14 C1
Seaton Rd ME7 17 H5
Seaview ME3 4 D6
Seaview Rd ME7 17 G3
Second Av, Gillingham ME7 18 A5
Second Av, Luton ME4 17 F6
Secretan Rd ME1 15 H6
Sedge Cres ME5 28 C1
Sedley Cl, Cliffe Woods ME3 7 F2
Sedley Cl, Wigmore ME8 31 E2
Selbourne Rd ME7 17 G1
Sellinge Grn ME8 18 D5
Sellinge Way ME8 19 E5
Selstead Cl ME8 18 D6
Semple Gdns ME4 16 C5
Setford Rd ME5 24 A5
Settington Av ME5 24 B1
Severn Rd ME5 24 A5
Seymour Rd, Chatham ME5 17 F5
Seymour Rd, Rainham ME8 27 E2
Shackleton Cl ME5 24 A4
Shakespeare Rd ME7 17 G4
Shamley Rd ME5 29 G3
Shanklin Cl ME5 24 A2
Sharfleet Dr ME2 10 C6
Sharnal St ME3 5 C3
Sharon Cres ME5 23 F6
Sharsted Way ME7 30 C2
Shaw Cl ME3 7 F2
Shaws Way ME1 16 A5
Shawstead Rd ME5 24 B3
Shearwater Cl ME2 14 C1
Shelden Dr ME8 26 B2
Shelldrake Cl ME3 4 C5
Shepherds Gate ME7 25 E5
Shepherds Way ME3 5 C5
Shepperton Cl ME5 24 A6
Shepperton Cl ME5 29 F1
Sheraton Ct ME5 28 D4
Sherbourne Dr ME2 11 G4
Sheridan Cl ME5 24 A3
Sheriff Dr ME5 29 E3
Sherman Cl ME8 25 F1
Sherwood Av ME5 28 D2
Sherwood Ct ME5 28 D2
Ship La ME1 16 C3
Shipwrights Av ME4 17 E6
Shirley Av ME5 23 E5
Sholden Rd ME2 12 A4
Shorefields ME8 20 A6
Short La ME7 18 C2
Short St ME4 17 F5
Shorts Reach ME1 15 H3
Shorts Way ME1 15 G5
Shottenden Rd ME7 13 G6
Sidney Rd, Borstal ME1 15 G6
Sidney Rd, Gillingham ME7 17 G1
Signal Ct ME8 26 C1
Silvan Glade ME5 29 E5
Silver Birches ME5 29 E2
Silver Hill Gdns*, Silver Hill ME4 16 D4
Silver Hill, Borstal ME1 15 G6
Silver Hill, Chatham ME4 16 D4
Silver Tree ME5 29 E4
Silverbank ME5 23 H4
Silverdale Dr ME8 26 B3
Silverspot Cl ME8 26 B3
Silverweed Rd ME5 23 F5
Sinclair Cl ME8 26 A6
Sindals La ME5 30 A4
Singapore Dr ME7 17 E2
Sir Evelyn Rd ME1 22 C1
Sir John Hawkins Way ME4 3 B2
Sir Thomas Longley Rd ME2 16 C1
Skene Cl ME8 26 D1
Skinner St, Chatham ME4 16 D5
Skinner St, Gillingham ME7 17 G2
Skua Ct*, Bligh Way ME2 14 C1
Slade Cl ME5 29 F3
Slatin Rd ME2 11 H5
Slicketts Hill ME4 3 D3
Smarden Walk ME8 26 D1
Smetham Gdns ME2 11 H4
Smith Rd ME5 29 E1
Smith St ME2 15 G1
Smithfield Rd ME3 4 D6
Snodhurst Av ME5 23 F6
Snowdon Cl ME5 24 A3
Solent Gdns ME5 24 A3
Solomon Rd ME8 26 C1
Solomons Rd ME4 3 C2
Somerset Cl ME5 24 B2
Sorrell Rd ME5 23 F6
South Av ME8 18 C6
South Bush La ME8 26 D5
South Eastern Rd ME2 12 A6
South Rd ME7 17 E1
South Side Three Rd ME4 13 F5
Southbourne Gro ME5 29 E1
Southfields ME1 15 H5
Southill Rd ME4 16 D5
Southwark Rd ME2 14 D2
Southwell Rd ME2 14 D2
Spade La ME9 27 E5
Speedwell Av ME5 23 F6
Speedwell Cl ME7 18 A2
Spekes Rd ME7 25 F4
Spencer Cl ME5 23 H5
Spenlow Dr ME5 28 D4
Spindlewood Cl ME5 29 E1
Spinnaker Ct ME1 22 D1
Spitfire Cl ME5 24 A4
Springfield Rd ME7 17 H2
Springfield Ter ME4 3 B3
Springvale ME8 25 G4
Squires Cl ME2 10 B6
Stable Cl ME5 24 A5
Stafford St ME7 17 F3
Stag Rd ME5 24 A5
Stake La ME2 6 C4
Stalham Ct ME7 30 C1
Stalin Av ME5 23 H2
Standen Cl ME8 31 F1
Stanford Way ME2 14 C6
Stangate Rd ME2 10 C6
Stanhope Rd ME2 11 G6
Stanley Rd, Gillingham ME7 17 G1
Stanley Rd, Wayfield ME5 24 A5
Staplehurst Rd ME8 18 C5
Star Hill ME1 3 C6
Star La ME7 24 D2
Star Mill Ct ME5 17 H6
Star Mill La ME5 17 H6
Station App ME2 6 C5
Station Rd, Cliffe ME3 6 B3
Station Rd, Cuxton ME2 14 C6
Station Rd, Rainham ME8 26 B2
Station Rd, Strood ME2 11 H6
Steadman Cl ME3 7 A4
Steele St ME2 11 G5
Steerforth Cl ME1 16 A5
Stirling Cl, Borstal ME1 15 G5
Stirling Cl, Park Wood ME8 31 F1
Stoke Rd, Hallows ME3 4 B3
Stoke Rd, Hoo St Werburgh ME3 9 G4
Stoneacre Cl ME8 25 H5
Stonecross Lea ME5 24 A1
Stonehorse Ct ME3 11 G3
Stonehorse La ME3 11 G2
Stoney Alley ME5 17 F5
Stoney Bank ME7 25 E2
Stoney La ME1 22 D4
Stopford Rd ME7 17 G4
Stour Cl ME2 11 F6
Stratford Av ME8 25 H2
Stratford La ME8 26 C2
Street End Rd ME5 24 A2
Streetfield Rd ME8 19 G6
Strover St ME7 17 F1
Stuart Rd ME7 17 H5
Sturdee Av ME7 17 H3
Sturdee Cotts ME3 9 H3
Sturla Rd ME4 17 E5
Sturry Way ME8 18 D5
Style Cl ME8 26 A6
Suffolk Av ME8 26 B1
Suffolk Ct ME8 26 B1
Sugarloaf Hill ME5 17 G6
Sultan Rd ME5 29 G3
Sun Ter ME5 29 E1
Sunderland Cl ME1 15 G5
Sunderland Dr ME8 26 C2
Sunderland Quay ME2 16 B1
Sundridge Dr ME5 29 E1
Sundridge Hill ME2 14 C6
Sunningdale Cl ME8 26 A4
Sunningdale Dr ME8 26 A4
Sunnyfields Cl ME8 26 B3
Sunnymead Av ME7 18 A3
Sussex Dr ME5 23 G6
Sutherland Gdns ME8 26 A4
Sutton Cl ME8 26 C2
Swain Cl ME2 11 F6
Swain Rd ME8 25 F4
Swale Rd ME2 10 C6
Swallow Rise ME5 23 H5
Swift Cres ME5 24 A4
Swingate Av ME3 6 B1
Swingate Cl ME5 29 F3
Swinton Av ME3 8 B4
Sycamore Rd ME2 15 E3
Sydney Rd ME4 17 E5
Sylewood Cl ME1 22 C2
Sylvan Glade ME5 29 E5
Sylvan Rd ME8 25 G2
Sylvestre Cl ME2 6 C6
Symonds Rd ME3 6 B3
Symons Av ME4 16 D6

Tadburn Grn ME5 29 F1
Taddington Wood La ME5 28 C3
Tamar Dr ME2 15 F1
Tamarind Cl ME7 25 F6
Tanglewood Cl ME8 25 G5
Tangmere Cl ME7 18 B3
Tanker Hill ME8 25 H4
Taswell Rd ME8 26 C1
Tatler Cl ME5 29 G3
Tatsfield Cl ME8 18 B6
Taverners Rd ME8 26 A3
Tavistock Cl, Lords Wood ME5 28 D4
Tavistock Cl, Rainham ME8 26 B3
Tay Cl ME5 24 A5
Taylors La, Higham ME3 10 C1
Taylors La, Strood ME2 15 H1
Teal Cl ME3 4 D5
Teasel Rd ME5 23 G6
Tedder Av ME5 23 H3
Telegraph Hill ME3 10 C3
Temple Gdns ME2 15 G2
Ten Acre Way ME8 20 A6
Tennyson Av ME3 7 E2
Tennyson Rd ME7 17 G5
Tenterden Rd ME5 23 H5
Terence Cl ME4 17 E6
Tern Cres ME2 14 D1
Thames Av, High Halstow ME3 5 A1
Thames Av, Rainham ME8 26 A2
Thames Vw ME3 7 F3
Thanet Rd ME8 25
Thatchers La ME3 6
The Adelaide ME3 7
The Beeches ME5 23
The Braes ME3 10
The Brook ME4 3
The Bungalows ME3 9
The Chase, Chatham ME4 16
The Chase, Rainham ME8 18
The Close ME1 16
The Common ME1 3
The Courtyard ME8 25
The Covert ME5 29
The Crescent ME4 13
The Crofters ME8 26
The Downs ME5 28
The Everglades ME7 25
The Fairway ME1 22
The Glade ME5 29
The Glebe ME2 14
The Goldings ME8 25
The Graylings ME1 15
The Green ME9 21
The Hazels ME8 25
The Larches ME3 10
The Links ME5 24
The Mailyns ME8 25
The Maltings ME8 26
The Mews ME2 15
The Mount ME4 3
The Old Carriageway ME7 30
The Old Orchard ME8 26
The Paddock ME4 3
The Paddocks ME7 25
The Pintails ME4 13
The Platters ME8 25
The Poles ME9 20
The Precinct ME1 3
The Queen Mother Ct ME1 15
The Ridgeway, Chatham ME4 23
The Ridgeway, Gillingham ME7 17
The Rise, Gillingham ME7 30
The Rise, Rochester ME1 16
The Sally Port ME7 17
The Shades ME2 10
The Spiers ME7 18
The Spinney ME5 29
The Spires ME2 14
The Street, Bredhurst ME7 30
The Street, Hartlip ME9 27
The Street, High Halstow ME3 5
The Street, Lower Halstow ME9 21
The Street, Stoke ME3 5
The Street, Upchurch ME9 20
The Street, Upper Halling ME2 6
The Terrace, Brompton ME4 12
The Terrace, Rochester ME1 3
The Tideway ME1 22
The Vineries ME7 18
The Wheelers ME8 25
The Whimbrels ME4 13
The Willows ME8 19
The Wirrals ME5 28
Theodore Pl ME7 17
Third Av,

illingham ME7 18 A4
d Av, Luton ME5 24 A1
lmere Cl, rindsbury ME2 12 A4
lmere Cl, illingham ME7 18 B2
tlebank ME5 29 E2
tledown Cl ME7 30 C1
mas St ME1 16 A4
mpson Cl ME8 26 C2
n Cl ME5 28 B4
ndale Cl ME5 23 E6
ndyke Cl ME4 23 G2
nham Rd ME8 19 E5
rold Rd ME5 17 F4
pe Walk ME8 31 E2
le Way ME8 26 A6
sh Cl ME5 24 A4
ston Dr ME2 11 E6
ry Rd ME8 19 H6
y Cl ME3 9 F5
ber Bank ME5 23 H4
ber Tops ME5 29 H4
agel Cl ME2 15 G1
agel Gds ME2 15 F1
uk Way ME5 23 G4
dington Cres ME5 28 B3
do Paddock ME7 17 H3
ate La ME2 11 H6
ey Dr ME3 5 B2
nto Rd ME7 18 A4
er Hill ME2 12 D3
n Rd ME3 7 E4
algar St ME7 17 G3
nways ME5 17 G6
son Ho*, he Fairway ME1 22 D1
ertine Rd ME5 29 E4
awn Cres ME5 29 F2
t Rd ME5 24 A5
ale Rd ME1 22 C1
ino Dr ME5 28 D2
ent Cl ME2 16 B1
ty Rd ME7 17 F1
wood Cl ME5 29 E4
ridge Rd ME3 9 F4
o Cl ME8 19 E5
or Gro, hattenden ME3 8 B5
or Gro, ainham ME8 26 B2
Cl ME5 29 F4
on Rd ME8 26 B1
bury Av ME5 28 D2
bury Av South ME5 28 D3
nan Cl ME1 15 H4
er St ME3 6 B2
stone Rd ME5 29 G3
can Dr ME5 29 F4
Posts Alley ME1 3 B4
gates Hill ME3 7 C4
dall Grn ME8 18 D5
dall La ME8 18 C6
ford Cl ME8 19 H6
r Dr ME8 31 F1
e Cl ME5 24 A5

erdown Av ME4 23 G1
on St, Chatham ME4 3 D3
on St, ochester ME1 16 A3
ury Way ME4 3 D3
hat Rd ME3 8 A5
ands Cl ME2 14 D2

Upnor Rd ME2 12 B4
Upper Britton Pl ME7 17 F3
Upper East Rd ME4 13 F6
Upper Luton Rd ME5 17 F5
Upper Robin Hood La ME5 28 B3
Urquhart Cl ME5 23 H6

Vale Dr ME5 23 E5
Valentine Cl ME8 25 E1
Valentine Dr ME3 5 B2
Valerian Cl ME5 28 C1
Valetta Way ME1 15 H3
Valiant Rd ME5 29 F3
Valley Rd ME7 18 A3
Valley Rise ME5 28 D3
Valley View Rd ME1 22 C1
Vancouver Dr ME8 25 H1
Vange Mews ME1 15 H3
Ventnor Cl ME5 24 A2
Vicarage Cl, Halling ME2 6 C5
Vicarage Cl, Stoke ME3 5 A6
Vicarage La, Hoo St Werburgh ME3 9 G5
Vicarage La, Lower Halstow ME9 21 G5
Vicarage La, Stoke ME3 5 A6
Vicarage Rd, Frindsbury ME2 11 H6
Vicarage Rd, Gillingham ME7 17 F3
Vicarage Rd, Halling ME2 6 A5
Vicarage Row ME3 10 C1
Victoria Cl ME5 28 B3
Victoria Rd, Luton ME4 17 F6
Victoria Rd, Walderslade ME5 28 C2
Victoria St, Frindsbury ME2 11 H6
Victoria St, Gillingham ME7 17 G2
Victoria St, Rochester ME1 3 C6
Victoria Ter ME1 15 G6
Vidgeon Av ME3 9 E3
View Rd ME3 7 E2
Viewlands ME5 17 F5
Viking Cl ME2 15 F3
Villa Rd ME3 10 B2
Village Vw ME5 17 G6
Vincent Rd ME20 28 A6
Vines La ME1 3 B6
Vineyard Cres ME8 26 D1
Violet Cl ME5 29 E5
Virginia Rd ME7 13 G6
Vixen Cl ME5 24 A4
Vulcan Cl ME5 24 A3

Wadlands Rd ME3 6 B2
Waghorn St ME4 17 E5
Wainscott Eastern By-Pass 12 B4
Wainscott Rd ME2 12 B4
Wainscott Walk ME2 12 B3
Wake Rd ME1 22 D2
Wakefield Cl ME2 14 D2
Wakeley Rd ME8 26 C1
Walderslade Rd ME4,5 23 F2
Walderslade Woods ME5 28 B2
Waleys Cl ME8 26 D1
Wall Cl ME3 9 E3
Wallace Rd ME1 23 E2
Wallbridge La ME8 20 C5
Walmers Av ME3 10 B2
Walnut Cl ME5 24 A3
Walsham Rd ME5 28 C4
Walsingham Cl ME8 31 E2
Walters Rd ME3 9 F3
Waltham Rd ME8 18 D5
Warblers Cl ME2 11 G6
Warden Rd ME1 16 A5
Wardwell La ME9 21 G5
Warlingham Cl ME8 20 A6
Warlingham Rd ME8 26 D1
Warner St ME4 16 D5
Warren Rd ME5 28 B4
Warren Wood Rd ME1 22 D3
Warwick Cres ME1 15 F6
Watchmans Ter ME5 17 G6
Water Works La ME8 25 G1
Waterloo Rd ME7 17 G3
Watermeadow Cl ME7 24 D4
Watermill Cl ME2 12 A5
Waters Pl ME7 25 E4
Waterside Ct ME2 16 C1
Waterside La ME7 18 B1
Watling Av ME5 17 H6
Watling St, Gillingham ME7 18 A6
Watling St, Strood ME2 10 C6
Watson Av ME5 23 E6
Watts Av ME1 16 A3
Watts St ME4 16 C4
Waverley Cl ME5 29 H3
Wayfield Rd ME5 23 G4
Wayweed Av ME5 28 C1
Weatherly Cl ME1 16 A4
Weavering Cl ME2 11 H3
Webb Cl ME3 9 F3
Webster Rd ME8 26 B1
Wedgewood Dr ME5 23 H3
Weeds Wood Rd ME5 23 G6
Well Penn Rd ME3 6 C3
Weller Av ME1 16 B6
Wellington Rd ME7 17 G4
Wells Ct ME2 14 D3
Wells Rd ME2 14 D3
Wemmick Cl ME1 23 E3
Wendover Cl ME2 6 D5
Wentworth Dr, Cliffe Woods ME3 7 F1
Wentworth Dr, Rainham ME8 26 A4
West Dr ME5 23 E5
West La ME3 4 B4
West Motney Way ME8 19 H4
West Rd ME7 17 E1
West St, Cliffe ME3 6 A1
West St, Findsbury ME2 11 H4
West St, Gillingham ME7 17 G2
Westbrooke Cl ME4 17 E6
Westcourt St ME7 16 D1
Westergate Rd ME2 11 F5
Westerham Cl ME8 18 D4
Western Av ME4 13 E5
Westfield Cotts ME9 21 F6
Westfield Sole Rd ME14 29 G5
Westmoreland Dr ME9 21 G5
Westmount Av ME4 3 B3
Weston Rd ME2 11 G6
Wetheral Dr ME5 24 A6
Wey Cl ME5 24 A5
Wharf La ME3 6 C1
Wharf Rd ME7 13 G6
Wheatcroft Gro ME8 26 B3
Wheatear Way ME5 24 A4
Wheatfields ME5 29 H3
Whiffens Av ME4 3 C1
Whiffens Av West ME4 3 C1
Whimbrel Walk ME5 29 G3
Whitcombe Cl ME5 29 F2
White Hill Rd ME14 31 E3
White Leaves Rise ME2 14 C5
White Rd ME4 23 G1
Whitegate Ct ME8 26 A5
Whitehorse Hill ME5 17 F5
Whitehouse Cl ME3 9 G5
Whitewall Rd ME2 12 B6
Whitewall Way ME2 12 B6
Whittaker St ME4 3 C3
Whyman Av ME4 23 G1
Wickham St ME1 16 B5
Widgeon Rd ME2 14 D2
Wigmore Rd ME8 25 F5
Wildfell Cl ME5 29 F5
Wildman Cl ME8 31 E2
Wildwood Glade ME7 25 F6
Wilks Cl ME8 20 A6
Will Adams Way ME8 25 E1
William Rd ME2 14 C5
William St ME8 26 C1
Willow Grange ME3 9 F5
Willow Rd ME2 15 F2
Willowbank Dr ME3 5 B1
Willowby Gdns ME8 31 G1
Wilmington Way ME8 18 C6
Wilson Av ME1 23 E1
Wiltshire Cl ME5 24 B2
Wimbourne Dr ME8 26 A4
Winchelsea Rd ME5 24 A5
Winchester Av ME5 28 D1
Winchester Way ME8 26 C2
Windermere Dr ME8 25 H4
Windmill Cl ME2 11 H4
Windmill Cotts ME3 5 C4
Windmill Rd ME7 17 F5
Windmill St ME2 11 H4
Windsor Av ME4 16 D6
Windsor Rd ME7 17 H2
Windward Rd ME1 22 D1
Windyridge ME7 24 D1
Winford Mews ME1 15 G6
Wingham Cl ME8 18 D5
Wingrove Dr ME2 12 A6
Winston Dr ME2 12 B3
Winston Rd ME2 14 D2
Witham Way ME2 15 F1
Wittersham Cl ME5 24 A5
Wiverhoe Cl ME8 19 H6
Wollaston Cl ME8 31 E2
Wood St, Brompton ME7 17 E1
Wood St, Cuxton ME2 14 C6
Woodbury Rd ME5 28 C4
Woodchurch Cl ME5 24 A5
Woodchurch Cres ME8 18 D6
Woodfield Way ME3 12 B1
Woodhurst ME5 28 B1
Woodhurst Cl ME2 14 C6
Woodlands ME5 29 E3
Woodlands Rd ME7 18 A6
Woodlark Rd ME4 13 E4
Woodpecker Glade ME8 25 H5
Woodruff Cl ME8 20 B4
Woodrush Pl ME4 13 F4
Woodside ME8 25 G4
Woodside Grn ME3 7 F2
Woodstock Rd ME2 15 G1
Woodview Rise ME2 11 F4
Woolbrook Cl ME8 20 A6
Wooldeys Rd ME8 19 G6
Woolwich Cl ME5 23 G3
Wootton Grn ME8 19 E5
Wopsle Cl ME1 23 E3
Worcester Cl ME2 11 F5
Wordsworth Cl ME5 24 A3
Wouldham Rd ME1 15 E6
Wren Way ME5 24 A5
Wright Cl ME8 18 D5
Wyatt Pl ME2 15 G1
Wykeham St ME2 11 H5
Wyles Rd ME4 16 C6
Wyles St ME7 17 G1
Wylie Rd ME3 9 F4
Wyndham Rd ME4 16 C6
Wyvill Cl ME8 26 A5

Yalding Cl ME2 11 H4
Yantlet Dr ME2 10 D6
Yarrow Rd ME5 23 F6
Yaugher La ME9 27 E6
Yelsted La, Lords Wood ME14 29 G5
Yelsted La, Yelsted ME9 31 G4
Yelsted Rd ME9 31 H6
Yeoman Dr ME7 24 D1
Yew Tree Cl ME5 29 H4
York Av, Gillingham ME7 17 F4
York Av, Walderslade ME5 28 C1
York Hill ME5 17 F5
York Rd ME1 16 A4

Zetland Av ME7 18 A6
Zillah Gdns ME8 25 G4

Edition 005 R 05.00